eco·craft

eco·craft

recycle · recraft · restyle

SUSAN WASINGER

An Imprint of Sterling Publishing Co., Inc.
New York

WWW.LARKCRAFTS.COM

Editor: **Kathy Sheldon**
Copy Editor: **Julie Hale**
Design, Photography, and Cover: **Susan Wasinger**

The Library of Congress has cataloged the hardcover edition as follows:

Wasinger, Susan.
  Eco craft: Recycle • Recraft • Restyle / Susan Wasinger.
      p. cm.
  Includes index.
  ISBN 978-1-60059-343-7 (hc-plc with jacket : alk. paper)
 1. Handicraft. 2. Recycling (Waste, etc.) 3. House furnishings. I.
Title.
  TT157.W3567 2009
  745.5--dc22

                          2008031192

10 9 8 7 6 5 4 3 2 1

Published by Lark Crafts
An Imprint of Sterling Publishing Co., Inc.
387 Park Avenue South, New York, NY 10016

First Paperback Edition 2011
Text © 2009, Susan Wasinger
Photography © 2009, Susan Wasinger

Distributed in Canada by Sterling Publishing,
c/o Canadian Manda Group, 165 Dufferin Street
Toronto, Ontario, Canada M6K 3H6

Distributed in the United Kingdom by GMC Distribution Services,
Castle Place, 166 High Street, Lewes, East Sussex, England BN7 1XU

Distributed in Australia by Capricorn Link (Australia) Pty Ltd.,
P.O. Box 704, Windsor, NSW 2756 Australia

If you have questions or comments about this book, please contact:
Lark Crafts
67 Broadway
Asheville, NC 28801
828-253-0467

Manufactured in China

ISBN 13: 978-1-60059-343-7 (hardcover) 978-1-60059-823-4 (paperback)

For information about custom editions, special sales, premium and corporate purchases, please contact Sterling Special Sales Department at 800-805-5489 or specialsales@sterlingpub.com.

For information about desk and examination copies available to college and university professors, requests must be submitted to academic@larkbooks.com. Our complete policy can be found at www.larkcrafts.com.

 This book was printed on recycled paper using agri-based ink.

To my grandparents
Fritz & Elizabeth Abplanalp
and George & Gladys Harris

Who spent all their vibrant and inspiring lives
crafting something from nothing but
imagination and ingenuity
and hope.

eco·craft
CONTENTS

turn green

I'm so tired of eco-guilt....Aren't you?

I'm tired of tripping over my big, ugly, gawky, clumsy, embarrassing eco-footprint. I'm sick of feeling bad and frivolous for being audacious enough to want things. I'm depressed by the not-so-subtle message that underlies the green movement. The one that hints that—all things considered—the best thing I can do for the environment is never to have been born at all. "Eco-conscious" basically means being endlessly *conscious* of what ecological disasters we humans really are. Green living is a minefield of "can'ts" and "don'ts." All in all, this eco-friendliness was making me crabby and really mean. And who can bear to live for very long in a hopelessly dysfunctional relationship with all the things you have and everything you are? Not me, so what to do?

Start where you are (with what you have on hand)

My first step to digging my way out of these mountains of guilt was to start being optimistic about life on this beautiful/graceful/powerful planet of ours. To put aside all the dour environmental predictions, and for a moment be hopeful and helpful and clever. I took a cue from my Swiss grandparents and my ancestors who settled in the American West. They knew how to make the tiniest things stretch a long, long way. No shirt would be thrown out before its fabric tidbits could find their way into a warm quilt. No chair would find itself tossed out when a leg got wobbly. No piece of wire, no old jar, no crust of bread was discarded without meditating on its possibilities. They used their hands and their imaginations as the power tools of transformation. So I decided to empower my own generation of possibilities. I started at the point of abundance, the potential of recycling and rethinking and reinventing the detritus of my modern life. Before I knew it, I had fallen, hard, under the power of trash.

Now I'm a re-psycho (and proud of it!)

This is a dose of environmental correctness that doesn't require me to sell my house and move to a teepee or trade the family car for a fleet of skateboards. I'm taking a break from worrying about all the things that have gone wrong, and I'm learning to do just a few things right: I'm making time to work with my hands. I'm making friends with castoffs and oddballs. I'm awakening to the preciousness of things deemed worthless. Every single day is full of surprises.

In the process, I have learned how to stake out a recycling center and shake down a junk store. I've learned to speak green at the home center and to put the natural back into my natural habitat. Most importantly, I've begun to look at my garbage with love and affection.

And in return, my mountains of rubbish have given me project after project—enough to fill a book!—of lovely/crazy/clever/fun things to make and to love. I hope you will be inspired to make them and love them, too.

This fey little glen was once an impenetrable tangle of fallen branches, rotting sticks, and leaf litter, until my favorite neighbors Bill and Deann Snider saw through the heaps of rubbish and started tidying up. They pruned, stacked, brainstormed, and imagined until they had created this magical, sculptural space.

THE ART (& craft)
of GREEN LIVING

CALLING IT ALL "GARBAGE" IS JUST PLAIN LAZY...

A tree adrift in blossoms is the ultimate demonstration of nature's bounteous overproduction. Waves of blossoms are produced in an attempt to create just one tree. But do we imagine the blossoms are waste or rubbish? No, we revel in this beauty and extravagance. Perhaps what we call the "waste" of human activity is actually a precious and beautiful resource waiting for its next incarnation.

ECO CONSCIOUSNESS-RAISING: When confronted with a pile of garbage, some bow their heads, some throw up their hands, some roll up their sleeves. Some—like architect William McDonough—don their nattiest thinking caps and change forever the way we define waste.

McDonough is a visionary designer/architect/writer who first postulated the "cradle to cradle" concept for a product. This is the idea that a product's creator could design for its entire life from initial use to what it might become after that. Inspired by the cyclical rhythms of the natural world, where the waste of one organism provides nourishment for another, he imagines that a product can have many lives endlessly reincarnating into the next necessary thing. In short, one generation of products becomes the food for the next—"waste equals food." With this simple/profound paradigm shift, he is challenging the notion that human industry must inevitably be a damaging burden to the natural world.

Hallelujah, what a liberating concept! Finally, a world view that doesn't cast humans as pariahs, hopelessly at odds with the planet. Finally, a vision that might actually welcome our environmental impact.

The idea that our garbage can become the raw materials for a new generation of useful, desirable objects is an electrifying—and dangerous—concept to those of us blessed (or cursed?) with itchy fingers. We crafty types who are ever eager to be making things, doing and undoing, reinventing, embellishing, and transforming—can we actually craft our way to a better world?

Eco Craft is an homage to the idea that there is a secret life in even the lowliest garbage. All that is needed is a little coaxing and crafting to bring it back to life and put it to work in our homes and lives. It is a practical renaissance—rebirthing, invigorating, and animating these humble and much-maligned materials. To use human ingenuity and imagination to create "life after waste" is the ultimate transformation, not just of our stuff, but of our way of thinking.

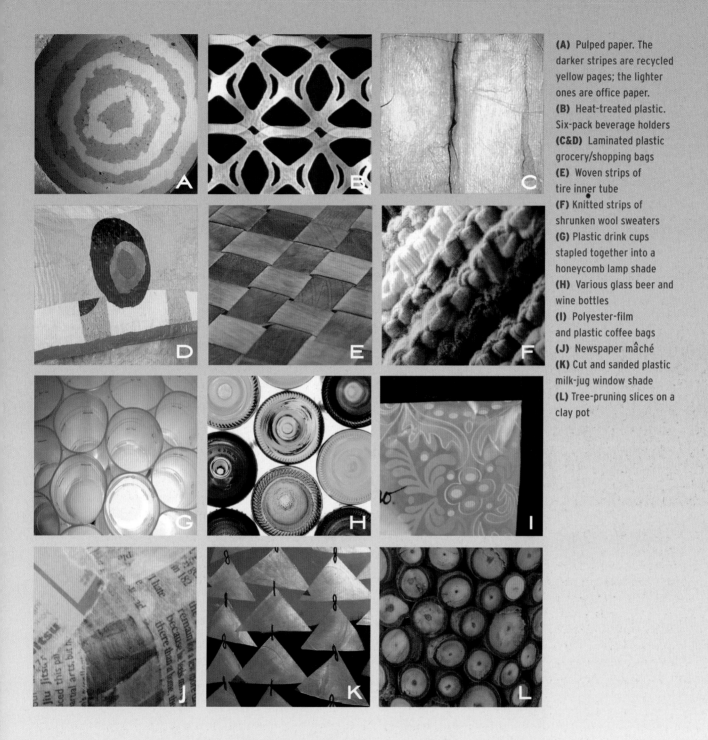

(A) Pulped paper. The darker stripes are recycled yellow pages; the lighter ones are office paper.
(B) Heat-treated plastic. Six-pack beverage holders
(C&D) Laminated plastic grocery/shopping bags
(E) Woven strips of tire inner tube
(F) Knitted strips of shrunken wool sweaters
(G) Plastic drink cups stapled together into a honeycomb lamp shade
(H) Various glass beer and wine bottles
(I) Polyester-film and plastic coffee bags
(J) Newspaper mâché
(K) Cut and sanded plastic milk-jug window shade
(L) Tree-pruning slices on a clay pot

*Design can eliminate the concept of waste,
producing perpetual assets rather than perpetual liabilities.*

WILLIAM MCDONOUGH
Cradle to Cradle: Remaking the Way We Make Things

ASSUME EVERYTHING IS REUSABLE OR RECYCLABLE

When you live three ferry-rides away from the mainland, you become acutely aware of the limited carrying capacity of a small island—and of a small planet. For the residents of the Gulf island of Hornby in British Columbia, watching mountains of their garbage chugging away on a ferry created a mandate for living lightly on the land. Thus, 30 years ago, the Hornby Island Recycling Depot was born. It is a phenomenally successful recycling hub where residents and visitors alike come to cheerfully sort and proudly sift through their garbage. Islanders quickly discovered that almost everything (from egg cartons to propane tanks to empty paint cans and used motor oil) can be recycled, and that there is precious little True Garbage. In fact, the Horn-a-bees are so efficient at recycling that they produce a third less garbage than the average North American, regularly recycing 70 percent of their waste stream. For the more rarified island castaways, there is the Depot's "Free Store"—the go-to place for the odd curtain rod, winter coat, sewing pattern, or bicycle wheel. The simple equation is to divide and conquer the island's trash, to organize people's garbage into something useful to someone else, and to keep island stuff out of someone else's landfill.

Divide and conquer

Life after trash

Plastic is flexible Plastic milk jugs render a material that is flexible, strong, and actually quite pretty when taken out of its utilitarian context. If you rough up the surface with sandpaper, it takes on a milky, sueded texture not unlike rice paper or shoji (check out the milk-jug shade on page 78). Plastic bags become a whole other animal when laminated together with a household iron. I've used this practical material to make everything from lunch totes, wallets, and day-timer covers to lamp shades (see pages 60 and 90). The polyester film/plastic hybrid that is used in lots of food packaging today (coffee bags being the most ubiquitous use; see page 42) is just too chic to be discarded. Plastic to-go containers are full of possibilities (see page 56). Watch out for interesting plastic packaging that can be retrofitted to another use, like the CD cases that turned into picture frames on page 38.

Glass is enduring Yes, it can be endlessly melted down and recycled, but it is worth finding ways to re-use it as is. Bottles and jars need not go back to square one: Check out the projects that repurpose them for practical storage (page 64), as an elegant light fixture (page 82), or as stylish decorative vases (page 20).

Metal really shines Aluminum from soda cans is an intriguing material with which to play. I once made a surprisingly beautiful holiday wreath from crushed, bright red soda-pop cans. But liberate the raw material from its "can-ness," and it can be cut, punched, molded, and stamped. It bends and folds beautifully, and it's the perfect material with which to "clad" a humbler material (check out the holiday ornaments on page 116). Tin cans are also endlessly practical for storage. What household doesn't have a can or two of loose hardware hanging around the garage? But if you want them to move into the living room, cans also make perfect bases for natural embellishment, as shown on page 34.

Paper takes many forms From newspaper to the yellow pages, office bond to old books and magazines, the possibilities for recycling paper are endless. You can fold it into something new and useful (see page 118), crush and wrinkle it to great effect (page 122), or mix it with water to make a great pulp to sculpt (page 30). Cardboard containers are just waiting for a new use—see what the classic oatmeal container can aspire to on page 74?

Salvage new life from old things

So many other castoffs can be given a new lease on life with a little imagination. Flimsy clothes hangers from the dry cleaners (page 66), old ratty sweaters (page 16), junky suitcases (page 68), prunings from the garden (page 34)—each of these finds a beautiful new life within these pages. And there are a few projects thrown in (pages 72 and 106) whose only purpose is to make your life a little bit greener.

DECORATE

Trash transformed...

Home decor whose beauty

is more than just

skin deep.

This rug is more than an inch thick, and every bit of it soft as a cloud. It's the perfect thing for your toes to encounter first when climbing out of bed in the morning. What makes it even more lovable is that it's made from 100-percent recycled materials using all-natural ingenuity.

SWEATER RUG

ECO-CONSCIOUSNESS GETS CUSHY This is quite possibly the fuzziest, thickest, squishiest, plushest, most huggable rug you will ever set foot on ... and you can make it yourself in a matter of hours. It's fashioned from back-of-the-closet, moth-eaten, out-of-style, thrift-store sweaters, washed and dried until the wool shrinks into a dense, comfy fiber. Cut these shrunk sweaters into strips to become the "yarn" you knit on big, fat needles, using the simplest stitch, into a delectably soft rug your favorite little piggies will adore.

METHOD recycle	material	TEXTILE	time **1/2** **day** or more
skill set: *knitting*			

MATERIALS

4 to 12 wool (or mostly wool) sweaters

TOOLS

scissors

size 19 knitting needles

sewing needle and thread

washing machine and dryer

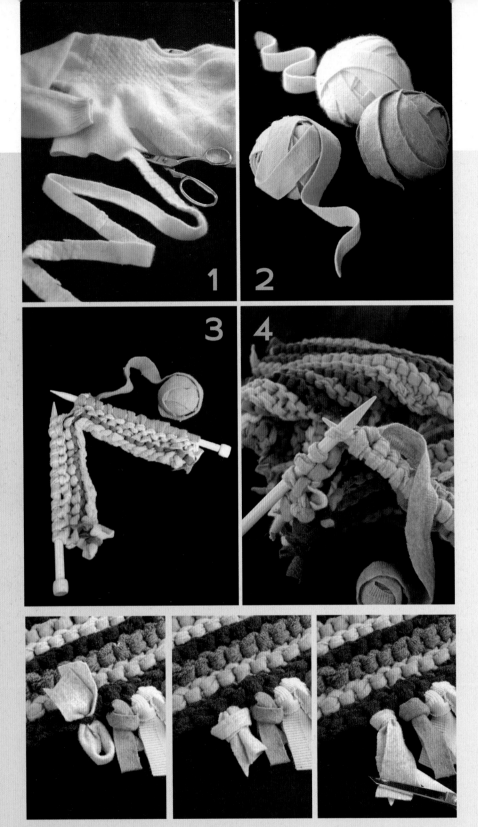

make it

1 Find old, 100 percent wool sweaters at thrift stores or in your own closet. You'll need four or five for a rug that is about 18 x 24 inches (45.7 x 60.9 cm). The larger runner rug shown here, which measures about 20 x 54 inches (50.8 x 137.1 cm), required about 12 sweaters. Machine wash the sweaters in hot water, then dry in a hot dryer. This process should "felt" the wool, shrinking it into a dense, tight, thick fiber that doesn't ravel or fray.

2 Starting at the bottom of the sweater, begin cutting a strip of fabric about 1 to 1 1/2 inches (25.4 to 38.1 mm) wide. Cut strips a little wider when the sweater fabric is thin, and narrower for denser, thicker fabric. Spiral up the sweater to make one continuous strip of "yarn" for your rug. Keep going until you hit the underarms of the sweater. You can also spiral up each sleeve as well to yield even more material from each sweater. Use a needle and thread to sew the pieces of yarn together into a long continuous strand. Repeat with all your sweaters.

3 Using extra-long, size 19 needles, cast on 20 to 24 stitches (for basic knitting how-to, refer to any beginner knitting book or knitting website). Work a simple stockinette stitch, changing colors to make a pleasing pattern, until the rug is the size you desire.

4 If you choose to make a longer rug, it can get quite heavy and unwieldy toward the end. Set the weight and bulk of it down on a table while you knit to make it easier to work the stitches. Cast off and weave in yarn ends.

Fringe 1, 2, 3 You can choose to create a fringe for your rug or not. Simply cut your fabric strips into 8- to 10-inch (20.3 to 25.4 cm) lengths, fold in half, and push downward through the stitches at the edge of your rug. Then push the ends of the wool strips back up through the loop that is formed and pull tight. Work across the entire edge, putting fringe in every other stitch. Even out the fringe by cutting straight across or at a rakish angle as shown.

For this rug, I knit two rows of each color before changing to the next. The photo on page 16 shows the "right side" of the piece, where the rows are fat and distinct. Here you see the "wrong side," where the pattern gets a bit more mixed up and jumbled—but in a retro, appealing sort of way. Experiment with colors and patterns of your own. Since these rugs are so fun and easy, you'll probably find yourself making one for every room in the house: the kitchen, the bathroom, the nursery, maybe even one for your favorite four-legged friend.

* The best recycled rugs are made using 100 percent wool sweaters that shrink tightly and make a dense, long lasting "yarn." If the label on your sweater says "washable wool" or includes some nylon mixed in, it won't shrink and felt in the washing machine and the resulting "yarn"—though still usable—won't be quite as nice. Other fibers that shrink and felt nicely are cashmere and mohair (from goats) and angora (from rabbits).

PAINTED BOTTLE VASES

Look for bottles of varying heights to
make a nice composition that gracefully
displays dried flowers, stalks of grass,
gnarled twigs, seed pods, and
even feathers.

VASE LIFT Wine and spirit bottles come in graceful, iconographic shapes, many too beautiful to throw away. Unadorned, the bottles look like someone forgot to take out the recycling. But, enrobed simply in a graphic paint treatment, the shapes come alive and strike an unusual balance between the primitive and the refined. The humble white matte paint brings out an obsidian sheen in the bottle-green glass and, suddenly, ordinary trash makes a leap to extraordinary treasure.

METHOD repurpose	material GLASS	time >3 hours
skill set: *painting*		

MATERIALS

green glass wine and beer bottles

masking tape

round stickers (or other appealing shapes)

white or cream-colored tempera or low-VOC interior latex paint

TOOLS

scissors

paintbrush

rubber gloves

1 **2**

3 **4**

make it

1 Collect glass beverage bottles of interesting shapes and colors. Remove the labels by soaking them for an hour or two in soapy water, then dry the bottles thoroughly inside and out.

2 Simple yet striking patterns can be applied to the bottles with masking tape. Create alternating bands of light and dark by wrapping tape around the bottle. This bold design was made by wrapping narrow strips of masking tape in random directions around the bottle. Wider tape will not adhere smoothly to the contours of the shape, so use scissors to cut the tape in half along its length. Remember that this project works in relief, so the areas you cover now will be the areas of exposed glass later.

3 You can also sprinkle round paper stickers on a bottle. Whether tape or stickers are used, they must be applied firmly with no corners sticking up to allow paint to get under them and obscure the pattern.

4 So far, this project has been a breeze. Here comes the messy part: Use acrylic, tempera, or low-VOC wall paint in a white or cream color. Do not thin the paint. Apply it with a small brush, being sure to cover the entire surface of the bottle. You may need to go over some areas twice to ensure even coverage. Next, holding the bottle by the top of the neck, pull the tape off slowly and discard it. The tape must be removed before the paint dries or it will pull off in large sheets and ruin the relief pattern. Be sure to have a trash bag handy for discarding the strips of unwieldy tape covered in wet paint. Rubber gloves are useful for this step, as you are bound to get some paint on your fingers. A craft blade may help loosen the edges of the tape or stickers to make removal easier. Once all of the tape is removed, set the bottles on a piece of newspaper to dry completely.

SIX-PACK SCREEN

This small three-fold screen stands about 5 feet (1.5 m) tall and stretches out to about 32 inches (81.2 cm) wide.

IMPROBABLE BEAUTY At first glance, a delicate Moorish filigree seems to adorn this folding screen. But look closer. It's simply made up of dozens of annoying plastic six-pack holders saved from the landfill. They're melted together with a home iron into a dramatic, geometric pattern. The resulting three-fold screen can hide an eyesore or divide a space. Impossible? No, just impossibly chic.

METHOD	material	WOOD & PLASTIC	time
rethink			1/2 day or more
skill set:	woodworking		

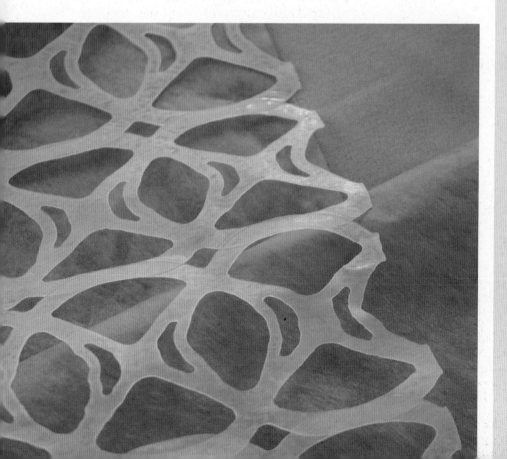

MATERIALS

40 plastic six-pack holders

6 boards of 1 x 2 pine, 6 feet (1.8 m) long

4 pieces of $3/4$-inch (1.9 cm) trim,
8 feet (2.4 m) long

12 wood screws, $2^{1}/_{4}$ inches (5.7 cm) long

four 2-inch (5.1 cm) hinges

$1/4$-inch (1.3 cm) brads or tacks

1-inch (2.6 cm) finish nails

water-based wood stain

TOOLS

baking parchment

iron

saw and miter box

drill

power screwdriver

paintbrush

hammer

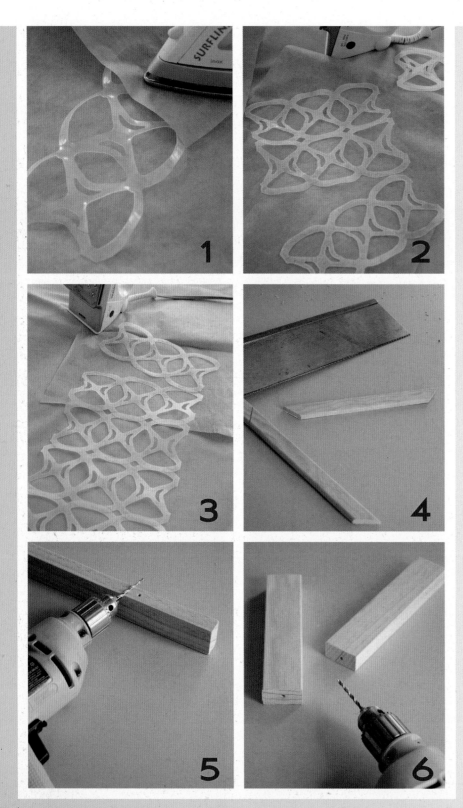

make it

1 Sandwich a six-pack holder between two pieces of baking parchment. Move the hot iron over the surface for about 30 seconds. Let the parchment cool until it starts pulling away from the plastic. Then gently peel the parchment apart. The plastic should become more opaque with an irregular surface. Repeat this step with all the plastic holders.

2 Overlap the bottom edge of one holder with the top edge of the next. Be sure to line up the sides so the pieces are even and square. Cover them with backing parchment and iron as you did in step 1.

3 Repeat step 2 until you have three sheets of plastic filigree, with each being one plastic holder wide by 13 holders long. The "fabric" pieces should be about 8 x 45 inches (20.3 x 114.3 cm) to fit properly into the wood panels. If not, adjust the wood dimensions in the next step to fit your fabric pieces.

4 Cut the wood for the panel frames using your saw and miter box. You will need six pieces of 1 x 2 pine for the side frames, each about 58 inches long (147.3 cm). Then cut six more 7-inch (17.8 cm) crosspieces.

5 & 6 Drill two holes in the sides of the long pieces: one $3^3/_4$ inches (9.5 cm) from the top and the other $48^5/_8$ inches (123.5 cm) from the top. Drill a hole in the center of each end of the short crosspieces.

You can use the "fabric" made from plastic six-pack holders for all kinds of things. It's perfect for obscuring or enlivening a view without blocking the light. Consider using it to create a very modern, tongue-in-cheek take on lace curtains. It also seems to be the perfect material for a lampshade, especially if you're willing to experiment. Try overlapping the pieces to varying degrees to discover all kinds of appealing patterns.

7 Line up the pre-drilled holes of the side frame pieces and the crosspieces. Drive the screws into place. Hold the wood flat so the panels are square. Once you have assembled the panels, measure the opening and cut your trim pieces to fit. Be sure to miter the corners at 45° angles for a tidy fit.

8 Apply the water-based stain to the wood panels and trim pieces. For this screen, I used a deep espresso color and applied three coats for a rich finish. Let the stain dry completely before attaching the plastic fabric.

9 Lay the plastic filigree in the opening in the wood panels. It should overlap the edge about ¹/₂ inch (1.3 cm) on all sides. Hammer the tiny tacks through the plastic into the wood to secure. One tack every 4 to 6 inches (10.2 to 15.2 cm) along all four edges should do the trick.

10 Nail the trim into place to cover the plastic edges.

11 Measure, mark, and screw the hinges into place, with two hinges along each adjacent side. For the three-fold screen to stand up properly, each set should hinge in opposite directions.

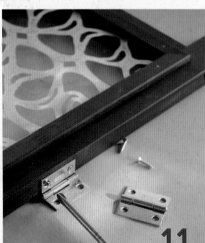

BOWLED OVER

METHOD **recycle**

material **PAPER**

skill set: *paper mâché*

time **½ day** or more

MATERIALS

yellow pages to recycle

used office paper

water

TOOLS

smooth plastic bowls to
use as molds

mixing container

blender or blender stick

strainer

knife or spatula

SCULPTURAL PULP Here's a recipe for successful paper recycling:
just add water. A short soak and a quick twirl in the blender turns recycled yellow pages and office paper into the wonderfully workable material used to make these cunning little bowls. The process is simple child's
play, but a little imagination and a graphic eye can transform common
trash into uncommon treasure.

1

2

3

4

make it

1 The paper is torn into inch-sized bits and then soaked in warm water for several hours so that it will soften. The yellow pages make a soft, sage green pulp, the office paper, a pale stone gray.

2 After soaking, use a blender (stick or jar-style) to whir the watery slurry into a smooth pulp with the consistency of a thick smoothie. Press the pulp through a strainer to squeeze out excess water until it's workable like clay.

3 For the mold, use a small, smooth-surfaced bowl without an articulated base (I recycled a plastic bowl from take-out). Form the pulp over the outside of the bowl, starting at the center with a little dollop, then working outward in bands of alternating color. Pat the pulp in place first with your hands then slap it with the flat blade of the knife or spatula. This smooths the surface, eliminates air bubbles, and works the separate bands into one continuous surface.

4 Let the pulp dry overnight. It must be completely dry, or it will be hard to remove from the mold. Use the knife edge to carefully loosen the dried bowl, then gently pop it off the mold.

To make this intriguing candle-holder, pulp is simply pressed over inexpensive glass votive holders and left in place, resulting in a delightfully textured surface.

Paper products are the largest component of municipal solid waste, making up more than 40 percent of the composition of landfills.

EMBELLISHED POT

SLICE OF NICE This is a simple and natural way to turn a humble vessel into an eye-catching piece of eco-décor. It's the perfect project to do right after the trees and bushes have had their yearly pruning. Cutting the wood into slices really lets its beauty and character show. A few thumb-thick branches can yield enough slices to cover a surprising amount of square footage. Be careful though—once you start seeing the transformation, no plain surface may ever be safe again.

METHOD
reconsider

material
PRUNINGS

time
>3
hours

skill set: *cutting and gluing*

MATERIALS

several small branches from trees or bushes,
ranging in size from 1$\frac{1}{2}$ inches (3.8 cm) to
less than $\frac{1}{2}$ inch (1.3 cm) in diameter

terra-cotta pots, old vases, or recycled tin cans

low-VOC, nontoxic glue

coarse sandpaper (to rough up metal or glass vessels)

TOOLS

lopping shears or any long-handled pruners

make it

1 Using lopping or long-handled pruning shears, cut the branches into slices about $1/2$ inch (1.3 cm) thick. You will need slices in a variety of diameters to cover the surface completely.

2 Start at the bottom of your pot or can and work upward. Dab glue on both the wood slice and the pot's surface to ensure a good bond.

3 Always dry-fit each piece in place first to ensure that it will fit nicely with the other pieces. You will be glad to have some tiny slices to fit into small awkward spaces.

CAN DO When using a tin can or glass as your base, rough up the surface with coarse sandpaper to ensure that the glue will adhere well to the surface. Glue wood slices on the surface as before.

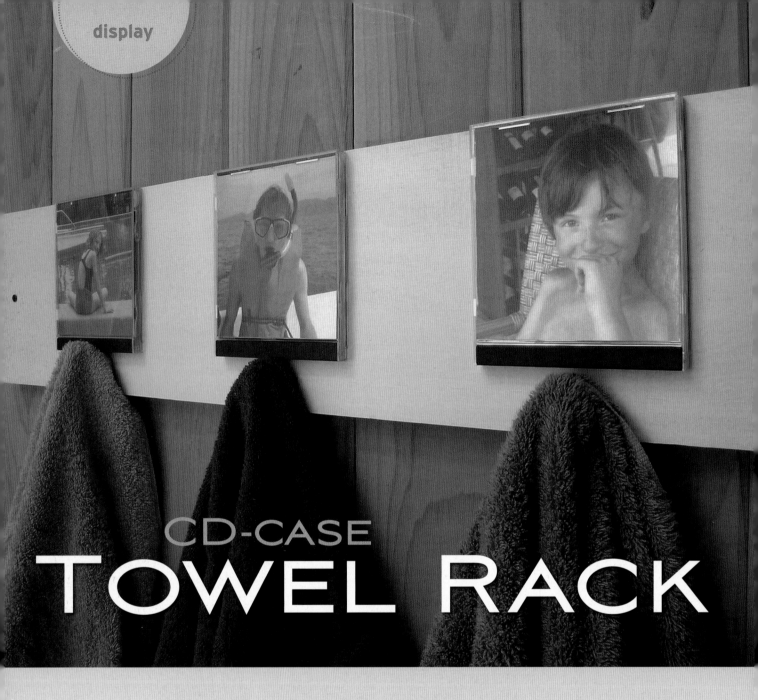

CD-CASE
TOWEL RACK

RACK IT UP Here's a clever project that does double duty. No, triple duty ... quadruple duty? First, it's a towel rack. Then it's a photo gallery for your family. Next, it recycles some of those pesky plastic CD boxes we all seem to have too many of. Last, it combines all of these things to solve a laundry problem. Personalize a towel space for each family member, and even kids will be more inclined to hang up their towels and reuse them for multiple baths. No more mess on the bathroom floor. Now you can put a face with every towel.

make it

MATERIALS

"jewel box" style plastic CD holders

photos

1 x 8-inch (2.5 x 20 cm) board, about 42 inches (107 cm) long

paint, stain, or varnish

exterior-grade mounting tape

handles, knobs, or hooks for towels

screws to mount rack to wall

TOOLS

straightedge

craft knife or scissors

paintbrush

drill

1 Remove all paper inserts from the recycled jewel boxes. Then cut black-and-white photos so that they measure $4^3/_4$ x $4^7/_8$ inches (12.1 x 12.4 cm) and insert them into the jewel cases with the hinge at the bottom.

2 Paint or stain the board as desired. Exterior-grade mounting tape works well for attaching the jewel boxes to the board because it's strong and resists water. Space the jewel boxes evenly down the length of the board leaving extra space at either end.

3 Align the top edge of the jewel box with the top edge of the board and press it firmly into place. Then drill holes for handles, knobs, or hooks so that you can hang towels under each photo. Mount the towel rack to your bathroom wall with screws at each end.

METHOD repurpose	material	PLASTIC	time 1/2 day or more
skill set:	*basic carpentry*		

CREATE

Practical, fun, clever...

ingenuity is at the heart

of these eco-friendly

necessities.

COFFEE-BAG TOTE

METHOD repurpose	material PLASTIC	time >3 hours
skill set: *cutting and taping*		

MATERIALS

about 10 to 12 metallic-looking 1-pound (0.45 kg) coffee bags

1 roll of duct tape, in the color of your choice

TOOLS

craft scissors

GIVE YOUR SHOPPING BAG A JOLT OF CAFFEINE Some people think it's silly to make bags out of bags. (My husband is one such scoffer.) But I just can't bear to throw away these beautiful, glinting coffee bags with one hand, and then shell out money for boring cotton shopping totes with the other. Instead, I build these urbane, chic, robust totes with duct tape and 100 percent post-consumer coffee bags. This project isn't hard, but it does take some time, some manual dexterity, and maybe the temporary assistance of another set of hands. So relax, brew a pot of your favorite (shade-grown) blend for you and a friend, and start taping!

make it

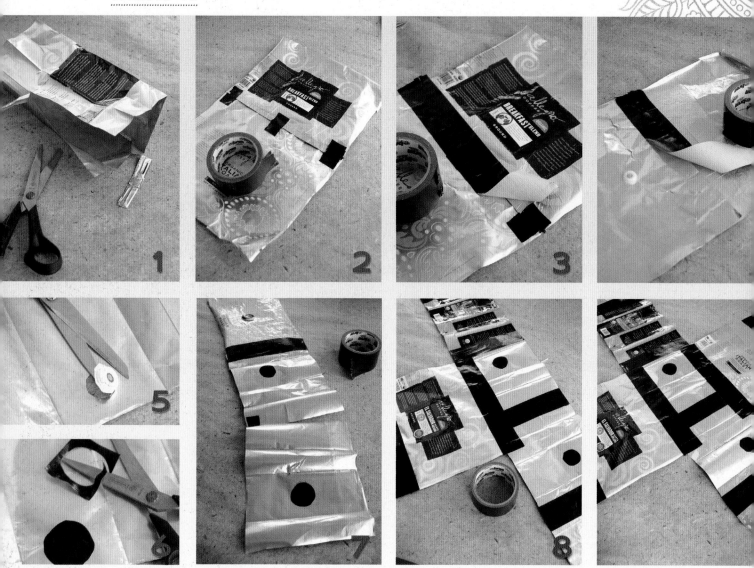

1 Cut the bottom off each bag and slice down the seam at the back. Our bags rendered sheets of material about 12 x 10 inches (30.5 x 25.4 cm).

2 Align and overlap the long sides of two bags by about 1/2 inch (1.3 cm). Tape the bags together with small strips as shown.

3 Tape the seam with a piece of duct tape. Go right over the strips used to tack the bags together.

4 Turn the bags over and tape the seam on the other side. Create two of these pieced sheets—one will be the front of the tote, the other the back.

5 & 6 Many coffee bags have a degassing valve you can remove if you want. Simply cut around the valve with your scissors. Then cut a round patch of duct tape and cover the hole on the inside and out.

7 To make the sides and bottom of the tote, start by cutting bags to a uniform width of 8 inches (20.3 cm). You will need four or five bags for this. Seam the bags together (as in steps 2 through 4) along the short side until you have a strip that is at least 8 x 48 inches (20.3 x 121.9 cm). This strip will extend down one side of the tote, across the bottom, and up the other side. Measure yours to be sure it goes the distance.

8 Tape the front of the tote to the middle of your long side/bottom strip. Seam as before.

9 Now tape the back of the bag to the side/bottom strip opposite the front as shown. Flip and tape the inside seams. Flip the tote wrong side up before starting the next step.

Many coffee bags are made of a shiny polyester-film laminate material. It is tough and long lasting, **but most recyclers won't accept it.** So make lots of these totes to **lessen the load at the landfill.**

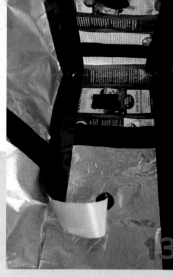

make it (cont.)

10 & 11 Fold the front and the right side-piece of the tote upward from the corner where they intersect until they meet at a 90° angle. Use small strips of tape to tack the front and side-piece together at the seam. Work upward along the seam to the top of the tote.

12 Tape over the seam, letting one half of the tape width go toward the front and the other half toward the right side. Repeat steps 10 through 12 to complete all the corners of the tote.

13 Open the tote as wide as possible and tape the interior seams.

14 To finish the top edge of the tote, fold duct tape along the perimeter.

15 To make the handle, cut two 15-inch (38.1 cm) lengths of duct tape. Press one into position running up the left side of the tote front about 3 inches (7.6 cm) in from the edge. It should overhang the top edge by about 8 inches (20.3 cm). Repeat this process with the second piece of tape up the right side of the tote front. Connect the overhanging tape pieces at the top to form the handle. They should overlap by about 1 inch (2.5 cm) or so.

16 Cut two more lengths of duct tape, this time each about 10 inches (25.4 cm) long.

Starting about 2 inches (5.1 cm) from where the outer handle meets the top of the tote, match up the new piece of tape to the sticky side of the outer handle tape and press together down to where they meet the top of the tote. Now continue to apply the tape down the inside of the tote and parallel to the outside handle. There will be about 8 or 9 inches (20.3 or 22.9 cm) of exposed sticky tape on the top arch of the handle. Repeat on the opposite side of the tote to make the second handle.

17 Fold the still exposed sticky tape in half on itself to create a narrower, finished handle. If you like, cover this with a piece or two of tape to soften the edges.

BAMBOO TRAYS

METHOD	material	time
rethink	BAMBOO	1 hour or less
skill set: cut and sand		

MIRACULOUS BAMBOO Growing up to three feet (one meter) a day, bamboo is strong, pliable, and waterproof. And sustainable. And did I mention beautiful? Cutting bamboo brings out its inner beauty and practicality. Cut it crosswise, and you can make lovely bud vases. Cut it lengthwise, and you can create beguiling, useful trays that bring the rainforest into your bathroom.

TRAYS Take your bamboo to a woodshop and have a professional rip it with a table saw. This isn't a difficult job, but it's better left to an expert, unless you're a hardcore woodworking enthusiast. I took my bamboo to a neighbor who builds furniture, and he took care of it in about 10 minutes.

make it

The segments in bamboo have thick waterproof membranes that separate the chambers. Using a handsaw, cut below them for a closed bottom, and above them for an open top. Lightly sand the bamboo pieces inside and out. Beeswax or orange oil can be applied for a nice finish.

For the bud vases, I used a shapelier member of the family called "Buddha Bamboo."

Bamboo is a grass, not a wood, and is **the fastest-growing plant on the planet.**
It can be harvested every six years, whereas a lumber tree can take 20 years.

INNER-TUBE BULLETIN BOARD

The rubber from inner tubes can be surprisingly beautiful once you release it from its mundane context. Powdery blue-grays are more characteristic of the inside of the tube; the outside is more of a uniform black.

Tire shops are often very happy to unload their used inner tubes on any takers. For this project, you don't need an inner tube that actually holds air, so you shouldn't have any competition from summer "tubers" to get the one you need.

TWO WRONGS MAKE A RIGHT Here's an idea for how to recycle two throwaway nothings into one very useful something: A bulletin board made with an inner tube and a piece of thick chipboard recycled from a wallpaper sample book.* This project is so quick, it might take longer to add it to your to-do list than to make it. But it will give that same to-do list the perfect place to hang out, along with other notable notes, inspired sketches, and shots of your favorite mugs.

* See other uses for wallpaper sample books on pages 68 and 122.

METHOD repurpose | material **RUBBER** | time **1** hour or less
skill set: *paint and cut*

MATERIALS	TOOLS
1 car- or truck-tire inner tube	craft scissors
grease-cutting soap	paintbrush
1 piece of thick chipboard	
low-VOC paint	

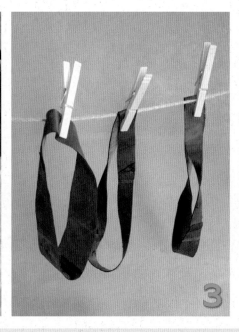

make it

I made these bulletin boards from the front and back covers of wallpaper sample books destined for the landfill. They measure about 12 x 18 inches (30.5 x 45.7 cm) and are about $^3/_{16}$ inch (0.5 cm) thick. If you don't have access to chipboard this size, buy thick matte board or small canvases from your local art store. Just be sure the board is stiff and firm enough not to buckle or curve under the pressure from the inner tube's rubber bands.

1 Paint the surface of the board with a paint color that will complement your room. One or two coats will be plenty.

2 With scissors, cut the inner tube into strips ranging from $^1/_2$ to $1^1/_2$ inches (1.3 to 3.8 cm) in width. You can slightly reduce the diameters of the bands by cutting them straight across the inner tube, or increase the diameters by cutting them on a diagonal across the inner tube. This ensures that they will fit snugly, but not too tightly, across the chipboard. Experiment to get it right for your board.

3 Wash the rubber strips thoroughly with a grease-cutting soap. Let dry.

4 Wrap the bands around the board at whatever intervals you desire to make a useful and aesthetically pleasing bulletin board.

The boards work equally well with the bands running horizontally or vertically. You can even try a combination of the two.

Bands that fit more loosely on the backing board can offer enough space to tuck in larger three-dimensional objects such as the pencils and seedpod above. The rubber is soft and forgiving enough to use with stickpins, small tacks, or even clothespins—for a bulletin board that can handle just about anything you throw at it.

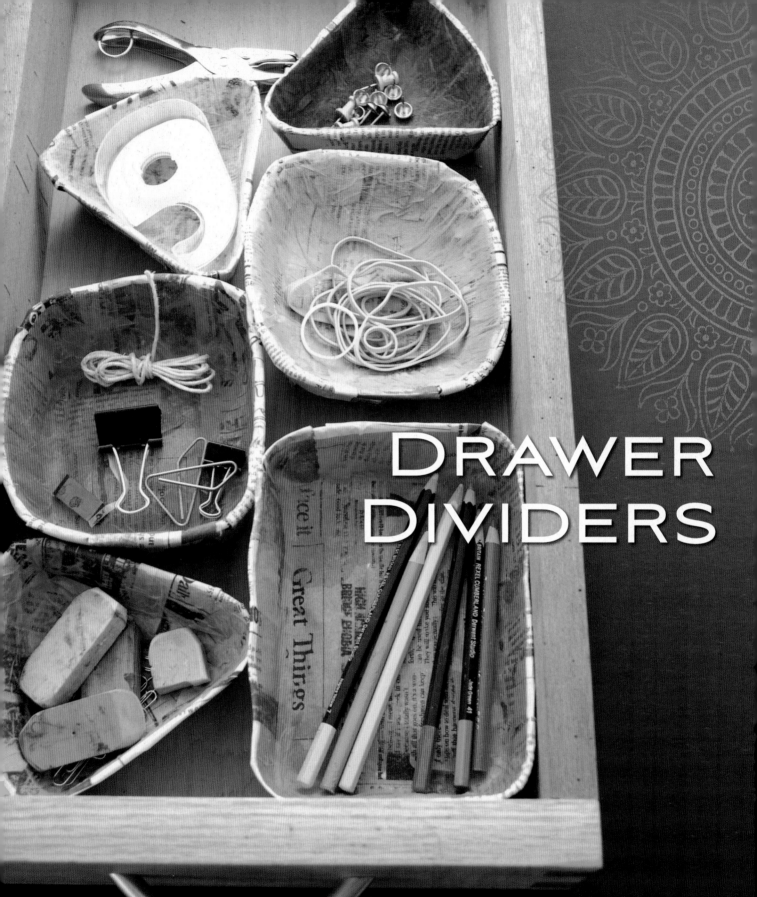

DRAWER DIVIDERS

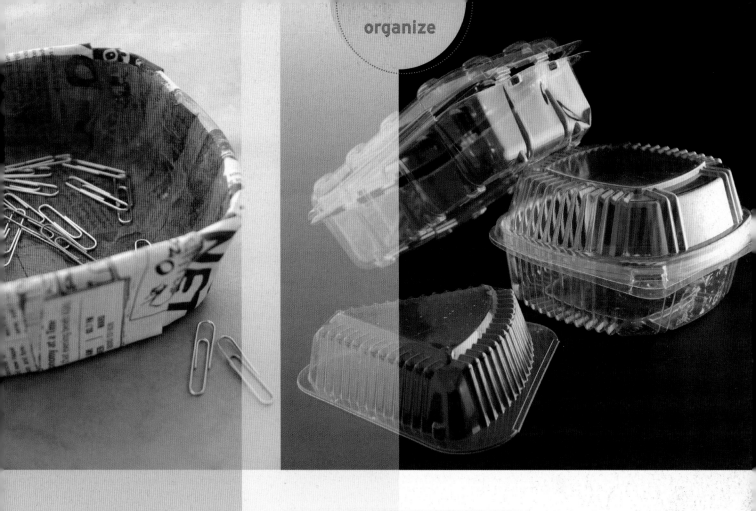

MATERIALS

plastic to-go containers

newspaper—find black-and-white pages for best results

colored tissue paper (recycle it from store packaging or last year's birthday party)

white craft glue

TOOLS

craft scissors

small paintbrush

mixing container and stirring stick

METHOD
recycle

material **PLASTIC**

time **>3** hours

skill set: *paper-mâché*

OPEN UP A CLAMSHELL TO NEW POSSIBILITIES It might be cherry tomatoes or maybe that piece of quiche-to-go from the deli, but if you're taking it home, it's likely you're taking home a plastic or polystyrene clamshell, too. Don't add the container to the landfill; recycle it into a perky little container to make a delectable drawer divider or delicious addition to your drab desktop. These dividers whip up in a jiffy and keep your junk drawer looking spiffy.

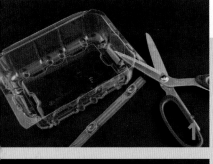

make it

1 Cut the clamshell apart where the lid meets the base. Trim around the rim of the clamshell, making sure you cut off the flanged edge at the top. This will give the container straight sides and ensure that the final paper-mâché piece has neat, smooth, rigid sides.

2 Tear the newspaper into strips that are about 1 inch (2.5 cm) wide. You can tear the strips into workable lengths as you go, depending on the size of your container and the part of it you're covering.

3 Mix one part white craft glue with three parts water in a container that's big enough to allow you to comfortably dip the paper strips. A recycled quart-sized yogurt container works well. The glue mixture should look like whole milk in terms of thickness and color.

4 Dip a strip of paper in the glue mixture, making sure you saturate it completely. Squeegee the strip between your fingers to squeeze off any excess glue. Drape the strip across the clamshell and smooth it into place. Cover the entire clamshell with strips going in one direction, then cover it again in strips running the other way. Make sure to press the strips down firmly, making contact with the entire surface of the clamshell, and squeezing out any air bubbles.

5 & 6 To cover the corners, use 2 x 5-inch (5.1 x 12.7 cm) strips of newspaper. Dip one of the strips into the mixture, then center the piece on one of the corners and tear the ends vertically into two narrower strips. Fold these narrow strips over one another to form a smoothly contoured corner. Use this technique for strips on the outside corners as well as the interior corners. To ensure that the end product is sturdy, the container should be covered with at least three layers of newspaper strips. Let the container dry.

7 With a small brush paint the interior of the container with the glue mixture. Tear colored tissue paper into pieces (about the size of tortilla chips), leaving one straight edge on each piece. Position the paper's straight edge along the top edge of the container and gently press it into place. Paint over the tissue-paper piece with the glue mixture, making sure you smooth out air pockets. Layer on tissue-paper pieces until the interior surface is completely covered. Let the container dry completely.

A plastic bottle or clamshell **will require 700 years** before it even starts to decompose.

DO LUNCH RIGHT

THE SACK OF SACKS No one knows exactly how many bags Americans throw away every year, but most estimates put the number in the billions. Those mountains of plastic shopping bags can take hundreds—even thousands—of years to break down in a landfill. Put those tenacious and ubiquitous properties to good use. Turn those trashy bags into a hardy, hip, seemingly indestructible lunch tote. All it takes is the household iron to meld layers of plastic bags together into a tough, flexible "fabric" that looks cool, wears long, and wipes clean. No sewing or gluing is necessary—the same iron that laminates the fabric melts the seams together.

METHOD reconfigure	material **PLASTIC**	time **>3** hours
skill set: *ironing & folding*		

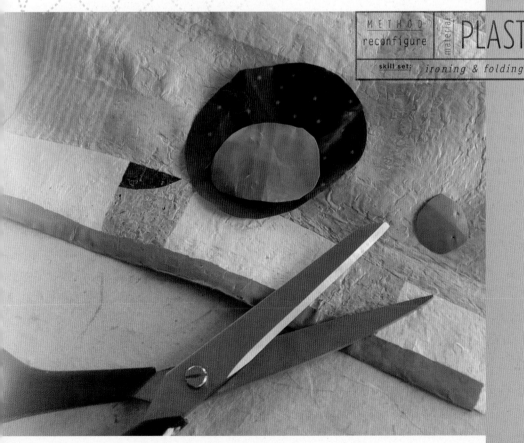

MATERIALS

plastic shopping bags

self-adhesive hook-and-loop tape

baking parchment

TOOLS

scissors

clothespins

iron

wooden ruler or straightedge

Anyone who's ever accidentally touched a plastic bag to a toaster oven knows that plastic melts quickly and sticks tenaciously. Laminating four to eight plastic shopping bags together makes the perfect weight of "fabric" for this unique, quirky lunch tote. The graphics on the shopping bags become transparent as they fuse and give the final product a subtle collage effect.

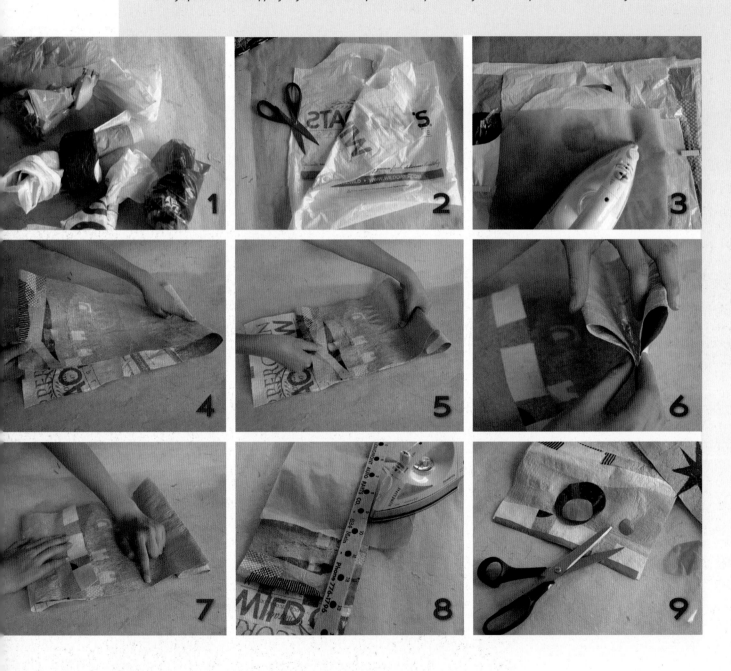

make it

1 Most plastic grocery bags are a little too flimsy for this project, so gather some sturdy plastic bags like the kind you get at your favorite clothing stores. Look for a pleasing mix of colors and graphics.

2 Cut the bags down the side seams with scissors and undo the bottom pleat to make a long rectangle of material. Four to eight bags layered together make a nice laminate, depending on the thickness of each bag.

3 Layer the bags one on top of the other and secure them with clothespins to keep them from shifting. Heat your iron to medium high. Put a layer of baking parchment over your ironing board and on top of the stack of plastic bags. Iron from the center outward, being careful to iron each section thoroughly for 30 to 60 seconds. Let the paper cool, then flip the whole thing over and iron the other side of the material. Let the paper cool until it comes off the surface easily and check the fabric to ensure that it's fully laminated. If it isn't, iron it again.

4 Trim your laminated plastic fabric into a long rectangle that's about 9 x 30 inches (22.8 x 76.2 cm). Fold the rectangle in half and crease the bottom edge.

5 & 6 Now fold down the front half of your material to create a rabbit-ear pleat or gusset along the bottom edge of the bag as shown in pictures 5 and 6. This pleat will create a nice roomy bag that can stand on its own. The excess material at the top will create the fold-over flap at the top of your finished bag.

7 Flatten and crease the bag into shape.

8 To make the side seams, place a wooden ruler or straightedge about $5/8$ inch (1.6 cm) in from the edges. The wooden edge will ensure that the heat of the iron melts together only the side seams and doesn't fuse the bag front to back. Make sure the top flap of your bag is open and doesn't get ironed into the seam. Protect your iron and board with parchment, then iron the seams together on both sides until they're completely fused. Take special care to iron the sides of the pleat, as there are several layers to fuse.

9 You can decorate the top flap of your bag by cutting fun shapes (stars, circles, words, initials, etc.) out of plastic bags and ironing them on. Take care to protect the other parts of your bag when you iron on the decorations so you don't accidentally fuse other parts of the bag together. Add a dot of self-adhesive hook-and-loop tape to close the flap if you like.

MESSAGE ON A BOTTLE

All kinds of jars and bottles can find a second life as practical storage in your kitchen or bath. Our favorite candidates include jars for baby food, salsa, and jam. Fancy beverage bottles can be reused for bulk oils and flavored vinegars.

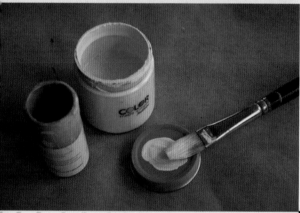

WRITE ON The surplus of glass bottles in need of recycling seems almost endless. Here's a practical way to reuse them a little closer to home. A swipe or two of blackboard paint turns old bottles and jars into stylish storage. More practical than store-bought canisters or jugs, these are containers you can write right on to keep track of what you have and when you need to use it.

METHOD recycle	material	GLASS	time 1 hour or less
skill set:		painting	

make it

1 Use the masking tape to define the area of the jar that will be your chalkboard "label." Press the edge of the tape securely to the glass to ensure that no paint will leak out and smear the line.

2 With a small paintbrush, apply black chalkboard paint to the jar or bottle. You will need to do two or three coats to get a solid black area to write on. Wait about five minutes or so between each coat. Remove the tape promptly after the final coat, while the paint is still wet. This will ensure clean lines. To remove any unwanted leaks or drips, use a utility blade or small paint scraper once the paint is dry.

3 Low-VOC wall paint in an eggshell, satin, or gloss finish will cover the old printing on the lids and ensure the containers fit with your kitchen decor. A variety of shades of the same color will make your jars spunky but tasteful (I used several greens like olive, lime, and sage). Paint the outside of the lid only. Don't put these jars in the dishwasher; they should be hand-washed gently when needed.

MATERIALS

empty glass jars and bottles

black chalkboard paint

low-VOC wall paint in eggshell, satin, or gloss finish

masking tape

TOOLS

paintbrush

utility blade or paint scraper

METHOD	material	time
Retrofit	JUNK	**1** hour or less

skill set: *drilling and tying*

HANGERS ON

BRANCHING OUT Wire hangers from the dry cleaners are about as uninspiring as it gets. But they can be given more style and even greater substance with a simple trick: Replace the cardboard bottom section with a length of branch pruned from a tree or bush. You can give the hangers even more practical and aesthetic panache by tying linen or hemp string over their wire shoulders to create a padded, slip-proof surface for your favorite garments.

MATERIALS

wire clothes hangers

hemp or linen string

tree cuttings

white glue

TOOLS

hand saw or loppers

drill

needle-nose pliers
(optional, for cutting or bending wire)

To cover the wire hanger, cut a piece of string that's about 3 feet (91.4 cm) long. Start by tying a simple half-hitch knot at the bottom of the hanger's left shoulder. To make the knot, the string will first go in front of the wire, then circle behind it and through the string loop on the other side (see photo A). For the next knot, the string goes behind the wire then circles around in front of it and through the string loop (see photo B). Pull each knot down firmly and push it tightly against the knot before it. Continue alternating half-hitch knots until you reach the neck of the hanger. Leave a length of string at the neck. Then turn the hanger over and repeat this step up the other shoulder with another length of string. When you reach the neck on this side, tie the two remaining strings together at the neck, dab the knot with white glue, and trim.

make it

1 The branches should be about as thick as your thumb and free of any loose bark. Nip off any branchlets, knobs, or buds. I tried several species of wood, including branches from a currant bush, an apple tree, and a long-dead cedar that still exudes a moth-repellent fragrance when cut. Be sure to avoid any wood that might ooze sticky sap. Evergreens like pine or fir would not be good candidates for this project.

2 Cut the branch to a length of about 15 inches (38.1 cm). I used a saw, but a pair of sharp pruners or loppers work just as well. Make sure the cut is clean and straight.

3 Remove the cardboard piece from one of the hangers, leaving about 1 inch (2.5 cm) of wire free for inserting into the branch. Drill a hole in the center of each end of the branch. Each hole should be about $1/8$ inch (0.3 cm) in diameter and 1 inch (2.5 cm) deep. Slide the wire ends of the hanger into each hole. Pressure should keep the wire in place. For a more secure fit, put a dab of glue in each hole.

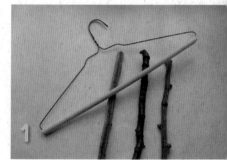

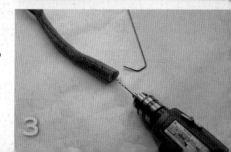

TRAY JOLIE

MATERIALS

old suitcase

2 drawer handles
with screws

large wallpaper
sample swatches

white craft glue

TOOLS

flathead screwdriver

needle-nose pliers

drill

craft scissors

METHOD
repurpose

material
JUNK

time
1 hour
or less

skill set: *deconstructing, gluing*

CARRY BREAKFAST IN STYLE Know someone who's in need of a little indulgence? You won't have to indulge at all to make this pretty, practical tray. It's fashioned from the top of a discarded suitcase and accented with handles from an old dresser. The tray is lined with durable wallpaper taken from an outdated sample book that came free-for-the-asking from an interior design center. Putting the whole thing together only takes about 20 minutes, leaving plenty of time for a leisurely breakfast in bed.

make it

1 Since wallpaper companies are constantly coming out with new designs, mountains of outdated sample books end up in dumpsters each year. Check under "wallpaper" in the yellow pages for sources. Most merchants are happy to see their sample books put to good use. Find old suitcases at junk stores, garage sales, or in your own attic. The hinges and locks needn't be functional, but the suitcase should be sturdy and have a flat bottom.

2 Separate the top of the suitcase from the bottom. All these vintage suitcases have different hinge mechanisms, so you'll have to be creative and use a little elbow grease to get them apart. If hinges are riveted in place, you can usually pop them out with a flathead screwdriver. Sometimes, as with the linen-covered case shown here, the hinges are held together by a pin that can be removed with needle-nose pliers.

3 Drill holes for the two handles on each end of the suitcase top. You'll need short screws since the side walls of the suitcase aren't very thick. Attach with a screwdriver.

4 Cut out wallpaper scraps from the sample book to cover the bottom of the tray. Wallpaper with a water- and stain-resistant vinyl finish is great for this use. Cover the back of the wallpaper with white glue and smooth firmly into place on the floor of the tray. Let dry. Then, bon appétit!

Here are a couple of other things that can be made from an old suitcase. No doubt you can conjure up a few more ...

AN IDEA THAT'S GOT LEGS!

Make a one-of-a-kind bench from an old suitcase by adding a set of furniture legs to the suitcase bottom and inserting a cushy upholstered pillow. These legs came off a sad, old coffee table and were easy to attach using metal brackets I found at the hardware store. Be sure to reinforce the inside of the suitcase with 1 x 4 (1.9 x 8.9 cm) boards to make the whole thing solid and sturdy. Have some upholsterer's foam cut to size for the interior, then wrap it in your favorite fabric.

STOP THE DRAFT

Made of easy-to-sew 100-percent wool felt, this draft blocker takes just minutes to make. It sports modern, graphic shapes of contrasting felt in four different colors on a black background. To make this piece, I used a pleasing and simple visual rhythm of shapes within larger shapes. But you can be creative and invent your own.

DRAFT EVADER Even the tightest, best-built house has places where cold air can sneak in. Under the door is a favorite spot and an easy one to fix. This colorful, hip, easy-to-make draft blocker looks nice doing its job, then folds in half and hangs so it's out-of-the-way but always-at-the-ready.

METHOD	material		time
retain	FELT		>3 hours
skill set:	simple sewing		

MATERIALS

$1/2$ yard (45.7 cm) of 100-percent wool felt
in black

12 x 12-inch (30.5 x 30.5 cm) squares
of felt in five other colors

thread to match

rice or sand for filling

TOOLS

sewing machine

scissors

spoon or scoop

make it

1 For the front, cut a piece of black felt about $3^1/2$ inches (8.9 cm) wide by the width of your door plus 2 inches (5.1 cm). For example, my 36-inch (91 cm) door needed a piece of fabric that was 38 inches (96.5 cm) long. Cut an assortment of circles, rectangles, squares, and lozenge shapes out of the contrasting colored felt. Make sure they fit on the black strip so there's at least $1/2$ inch (1.3 cm) at the top and bottom. Sew the shapes onto the black background felt using a machine or by hand.

2 & 3 For the back, cut another strip of felt in a contrasting color (here, loden green) that's about 1 inch (2.5 cm) wider and longer than the black piece. Line up the black front on top of the contrasting back, leaving about $1/2$ inch (1.3 cm) of the back fabric exposed all around the edges. Machine-sew all the way around, leaving the top edge open to add the filling.

4 You can fill your draft stopper with a variety of materials. Sand works well, although it's a bit heavy. I used about two to three cups of rice for this one. You can also try dried lentils or coarse cornmeal. Do not overfill the piece. The filling is meant to plump up the stopper and make it just heavy enough to stay put. Machine-sew the end closed.

5 The handles are simply pieces of felt measuring about 7 x 2 inches (17.8 x 5.1 cm). The felt pieces should be folded in half and then sewn. Attach them to each end of the stopper, using a double row of machine-stitching for strength.

CAN BE BEAUTIFUL

METHOD recycle | material FIBERBOARD | time 1 hour or less

skill set: cutting and gluing

MATERIALS

decorative papers

fiberboard food containers

white craft glue

cork lids or coasters

wine corks

wood screws

oversized, black rubber washers (optional)

TOOLS

scissors

small paintbrush

IN THE CAN Stow away kitchen stuff like tea bags and dry pasta—maybe even your secret cash stash—with these natty little canisters. They're uptown enough for the top shelf, but they have humble beginnings as packaging for oatmeal, raisins, and sea salt. Specialty bookmaking papers, wrapping paper, origami paper, old maps, and playbills can all be mixed and matched to make surprisingly elegant, super-simple storage.

make it

1 Try your local art supply or stationery store for interesting papers. Make sure the paper is thick enough so that it doesn't become transparent when glued.

2 Cut your paper to wrap around the cylinder with an overlap of about ¹/₂ inch (1.3 cm). For packages with a cardboard edge, cut the paper 1 inch (2.5 cm) taller than the height of the cylinder so the paper can be folded over the top. For those with metal edges, cut the paper to fit between the metal rims at the top and bottom of the container. Brush the wrong side of the paper with diluted white glue or paste. Then position the paper so that it's even with the bottom edge and press it around the cylinder, smoothing out wrinkles as you go. Burnish the paper firmly with the heel of your hand.

3 Clip the overhanging paper so that it's perpendicular to the canister edge to make folding tabs. If necessary, brush the tabs with a little extra glue before folding them down into the canister.

4 Cork coasters work perfectly for the lids. Or you can purchase cork lids at a hardware or houseware store. Thread a wood screw up through the bottom of the coaster, then wind a wine cork onto the screw until it's finger-tight. You can use the optional, oversized black rubber washers for a decorative finish.

For interesting paper, try your local art supply or stationery store, but don't overlook the recycling bin for possibilities. Just make sure the paper is thick enough so that it doesn't become transparent when glued.

ILLUMINATE

Mood-setting illumination...

Lighting ideas can be eco-conscious

and surprisingly beautiful.

MILK-JUG
PENDANT

The sanded plastic looks like a hardy version of Japanese rice-paper shoji. The organic shape hints at a tulip, a seedpod, or a glowworm and works just as well in a traditional setting as it does in a modern one. It's perfect for illuminating a dining room or kitchen.

SHED A NEW LIGHT ON AN OLD PROBLEM Plastic milk jugs—millions of them—enter the waste stream every year. They're big, ugly, and, well, very trashy. So who would've thought you could make a stylish, mid-century-mod pendant shade that would keep six jugs out of the dumpster? The semi-translucent shade softens the glow of compact fluorescent bulbs and looks almost like a silky cocoon or, perhaps more appropriately, like milk glass from the last century. The assembly is a snap. I used office staples and bamboo skewers to hold it all together. These honest, no-nonsense materials give the shade an edgy, industrial attitude that dares anyone to question its humble origins.

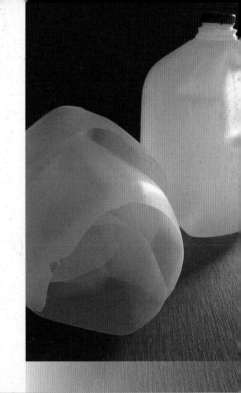

METHOD **rethink** | material PLASTIC | time >3 hours

skill set: *cut and staple*

MATERIALS

6 translucent, gallon-sized milk jugs

six bamboo skewers, each 12 inches (30.5 cm)

one pendant light socket with cord and fluorescent bulb

TOOLS

scissors or utility knife

medium-grade sandpaper

stapler

small hole punch

clippers to cut skewers

access to a photocopier

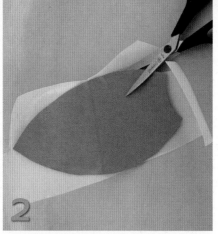

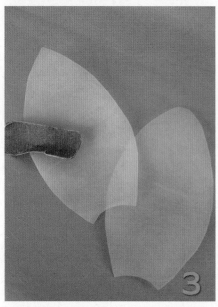

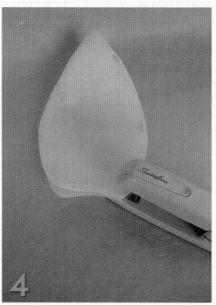

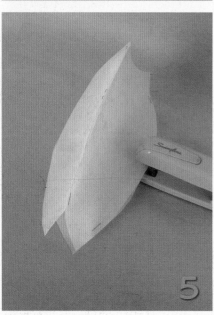

make it

Collect six clean gallon containers. Some plastic jugs have a circular depression on the front or side for stability. This type will NOT work for this project. You need jugs that have large areas of smooth plastic for cutting out 6 x 11-inch (15.2 x 27.9 cm) petal-shaped panels.

1 Create a template, using the pattern and instructions on the opposite page. Using a utility knife or scissors, and the template on the opposite page as a guide, cut a large expanse of mostly smooth plastic from the front, sides, and shoulders of the plastic jug.

2 Tape the template on the plastic and cut out the shape. Mark the position for the punched hole at the top. Do this with six jugs. The plastic will seem a little stiff at this point, but you can make it more pliable by rolling and unrolling it several times in both directions to soften it.

3 Using medium-grade sandpaper, create tight swirls in the surface of both sides of the petal-shaped pieces. The sanding will further soften the plastic. Wash any plastic dust off the pieces.

4 Staple two of the petals together in three places as shown. Put the staples about $1/4$ inch (0.6 cm) in from the edge.

5 Gently open up the two pieces and fit another piece to one edge, aligning it top to bottom. Then staple again in three places. It's easiest to start with the middle staple.

6 Continue stapling new pieces to the shade until you've attached all six pieces. Then close the shade by stapling the first piece to the last piece.

✳ Compact fluorescent bulbs are the smart choice and the safe one. They don't dissipate energy in the form of heat, so they use energy more efficiently and virtually eliminate any risk of fire.

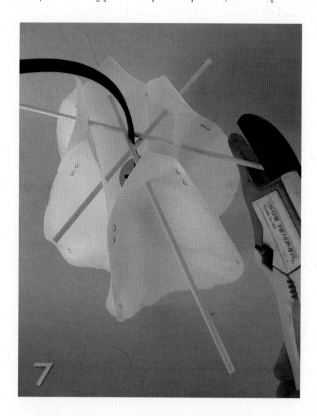

Trace this pattern and photocopy it at 200 percent to make a template that is approximately 6 x 11 inches (15.2 x 27.9 cm). Use 8 $\frac{1}{2}$ x 14-inch (21.5 x 35.5 cm) copy paper. Cut out the template and use it to cut six pieces of plastic for your lamp.

Use a smallish hole punch to create a hole in the top of each panel in the position shown on the template. The holes should be big enough to accommodate your bamboo skewers but small enough so that the skewers don't slip around in the hole. Alternatively, you can cut two short lines that cross in the middle—like plus signs—for the bamboo to go through.

7 You'll need a standard pendant light fixture—basically, just a cord with a socket attached. To hang the shade over the fixture, thread a bamboo skewer through the hole on one side of the shade and the hole directly opposite. Put the cord next to this skewer, then thread another skewer through the adjacent hole and through the hole opposite. The cord will now be sitting in a V-shaped notch created by the two skewers. Thread the last skewer through; it will secure the cord in place. Then cut the skewers to the desired lengths with a pair of garden clippers or scissors.

If every American household recycled just one out of every ten HDPE bottles or containers used, it would keep **200 million pounds of plastic out of landfills.**

Although this chandelier is a visual feast, I crafted it from the humblest and least expensive materials. Aside from a few nuts and bolts, all the materials here were either salvaged or recycled, making it truly the "priceless" relic it appears to be.

BABY-JAR CHANDELIER

LIGHTEN UP THE RECYCLING Take the baby jars out of the waste stream and give them a higher purpose. This stunning chandelier has all the charm and character of medieval ironwork—no one ever needs to know that it comes from the recycling bin instead of some far-flung castillo. A few yards of twisted wire, a couple of repurposed barrel hoops, and a length of rusty chain are all it takes to spark images of exotic locales. Powered by 18 votive candles, the chandelier twinkles with light and crackles with electricity without drawing a single watt.

MATERIALS

tie wire

18 baby food jars

18 votive or tealight candles

2 barrel hoops

6 eyehook bolts (black or rusty, if possible)

12 nuts to match the bolts

about 9 feet (2.7 m) of lightweight chain (dark or rusty, if possible)

large S-hook

TOOLS

wire cutters

needle-nose pliers

jigsaw with metal-cutting blade for barrel hoops (if needed)

clamp

drill

METHOD	material	time
rethink	GLASS	1/2 day or more
skill set:	twisting wire	

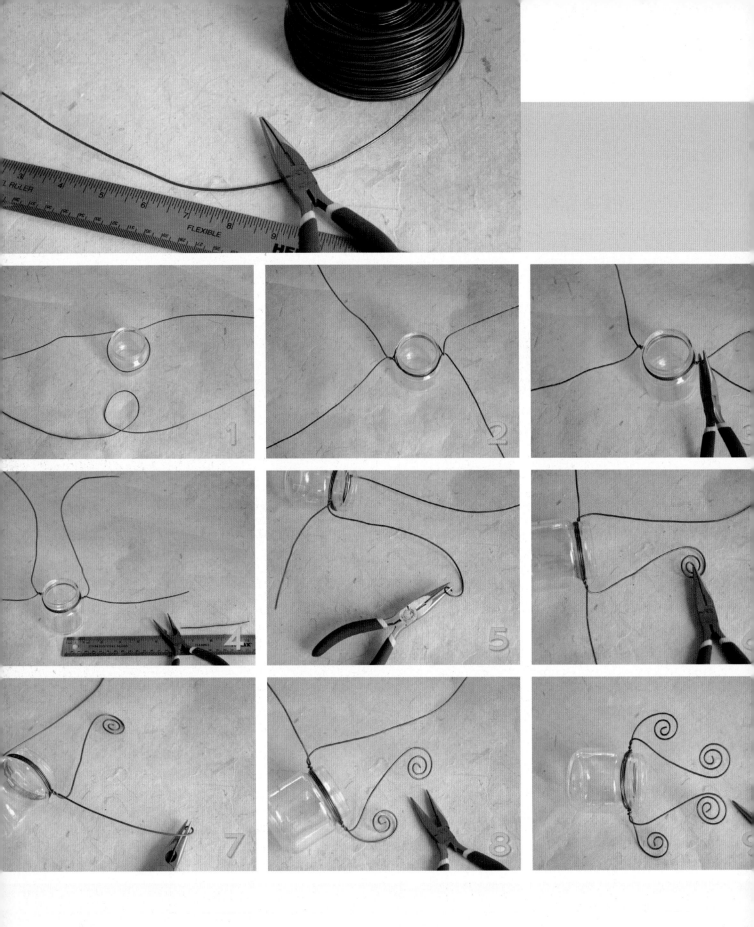

make it

1 Measure and cut two 24-inch (61 cm) lengths of tie wire. Make a loop in the center of each wire. Place one loop over the neck of the baby food jar and tighten slightly. Then put the other loop over the neck, going in the opposite direction so the points where the wires cross in the loops are on opposite sides of the jar neck. Cinch down.

2 Pulling the loops as tightly as possible, twist the end wires around each other to secure the wire on the neck of the jar.

3 Hold the twists in the needle-nose pliers and give them two more firm twists to tighten the loops completely on the neck.

4 Bend the lower wire on each side up so it shoots straight up from the jar. This wire should measure about 8 inches (20.3 cm), so cut it if necessary. Bend the other two wires out horizontally from the jar. Cut these to be about 5 inches (12.7 cm) long.

5 Grab the tip of the upper wire and curl it slowly outward to form a spiral. The first curl should be very tight. The curl should then loosen as you continue spiraling.

6 The finished spiral should be about 1 inch (2.5 cm) across and have about three twists. The spirals for the upper wires should turn outward as shown here.

7 & 8 The spirals for the shorter, lower wires should be about the same size as the ones above, but they should curl inward this time.

9 Repeat the spirals on the two remaining wires to make a symmetrical holder.

At this point, you could just stop here and use this wire-topped jar as the adorable votive holder shown above. If, however, you have been seduced by the more grandiose, jaw-dropping chandelier, do press on....

Once you have mastered the technique and finished one of these candleholders, the subsequent ones will take only about five minutes. Making the 18 that are necessary for this chandelier is not a lifetime's work—it should take a couple of hours or so. Consider making it a rainy-weekend project.

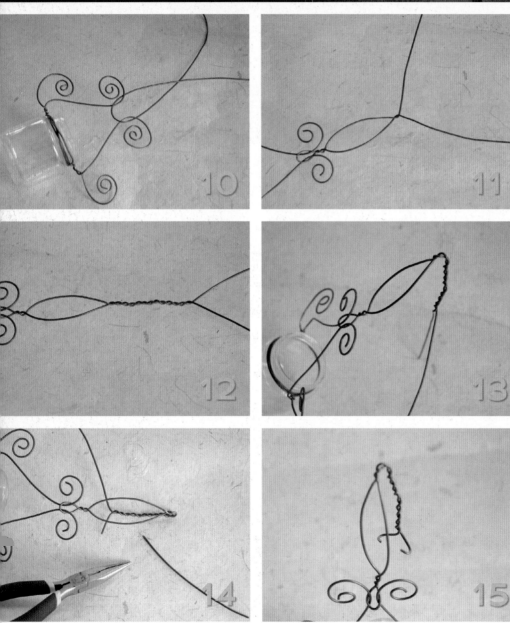

make it (cont.)

10 Cut a 20-inch (50.8 cm) piece of wire and make a loose loop in its center. Then loop it over the two top spirals on the jar so it grabs the necks of the two spirals as shown.

11 With the pliers, make three tight twists at the neck of the loop. Then create a large oval about 3 inches (7.6 cm) long. Twist to close the oval.

12 With the needle-nose pliers, make 12 to 14 twists in the two wires or however many twists are required to measure 3 inches (7.6 cm).

13 Use the pliers to bend the twisted portion down as shown in the photo. Leave a few inches of wire beyond the twists.

14 Bend the remaining wire ends into 90° angles. Then cut each end so that about 1 inch (2.5 cm) of wire extends beyond the bend.

15 Make a small hook on the end of each wire. The hooks should face forward. They clasp onto the wire loop to lock the candleholder to the hoop of the chandelier.

SET UP Now that you have made the candleholders, it is time to move on to the structural base of the chandelier. It is a simple structure with two hoops; the top hoop has a smaller diameter than the bottom one. Three pieces of 36-inch (91.4 cm) chain connect them. The three lengths of chain join at the top in an S-hook from which the chandelier hangs.

I made this chandelier using two steel hoops from a decrepit oak half-barrel planter that I bought several years ago from a home center. It had weathered many Colorado winters before the wood finally broke down and the hoops slipped off. Most of these barrel planters seem to share this fate, so hoops shouldn't be hard to find. You will likely need to cut one or both hoops down to size. Cutting through the hoop steel with a hacksaw is painfully slow work. Instead, use a jigsaw fitted with a metal blade. I must admit that I hired a local tough-guy to do this cut for me, but you can do it yourself if you are so inclined. The diameter of one hoop should measure 17 inches (43.2 cm) and the other 24 inches (61 cm), but be sure to add an extra 4 inches (10.2 cm) so the metal ends overlap at the joint.

16 Clamp the overlapping ends of the metal hoop to your work surface and drill a hole through both layers.

17 Thread a nut onto the neck of the eyehook bolt, and then push the bolt through the hole in the metal. Fasten the second nut on the end of the bolt to sandwich together the two layers of hoop.

18 Measure the circumference of your circular hoop and divide that number by three. Drill holes in the hoop at those one-third intervals and affix an eyehook bolt at each position. The chains attach to these bolts.

19 Insert a link through the eye of the bolt to attach the chain to the bottom hoop.

20 To attach the top hoop, thread the head of the bolt through the link in the chain.

21 All three chains meet at the top in an S-hook from which the chandelier hangs.

grocery bag SHADE

MATERIALS

10 to 15 flimsy plastic grocery shopping bags, 4 beige, the rest white

8 sturdy bamboo skewers each at least 1 foot (30.5 cm) long

2 feet (61 cm) of lightweight twine or fine wire

lamp socket with cord

fluorescent bulb

bamboo skewers

TOOLS

scissors

towel to cover work surface

baking parchment

iron

metal ruler or straightedge

craft blade or box cutter

SEE PLASTIC BAGS IN A WHOLE NEW LIGHT We all know how disastrous plastic shopping bags are for the environment. They're tacky, ugly—sometimes even lethal—litter. Here's a project that takes a few of those wayward bags off the streets and puts them to work on improving the environment—the home environment, that is. This beautiful, earthy pendant lampshade is made of nothing more than used shopping bags—the flimsy kind you get from the grocery store. The secret? Apply a little heat to laminate the plastic bags into a textural, translucent "fabric" that seems like something organic—tree bark or animal hide—instead of plastic. With a few deft folds, this project casts those humble little bags into a light that even Noguchi might find illuminating.

METHOD recreate | material PLASTIC | skill set: ironing | time >3 hours

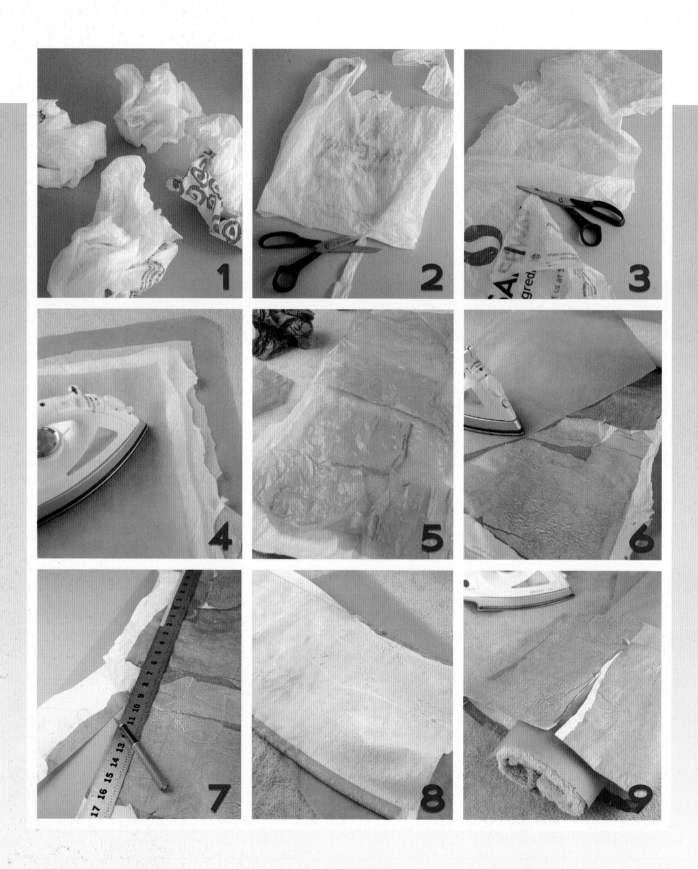

make it

1 Gather your plastic shopping bags. Use the flimsy kind from the grocery store. You'll need white ones as well as beige ones.

2 & 3 Cut off the bottom seam and the handles of a bag with scissors. Then cut off the printed area of the bag to create as large an expanse as possible of clean, unprinted plastic. You should cut the side of the bag close to the printing. Repeat with the rest of the white and beige bags.

4 Cover your work surface with a towel, then lay down a sheet of baking parchment to keep the heated plastic from sticking. Heat the iron to medium high. To create a base layer for the project, lay down a sheet of white plastic bag with another piece next to it so that the sheets overlap by a couple of inches. Depending on the size of your bags, you may need to put together more pieces to create a base of about 14 x 36 inches (35.6 x 91.4 cm). Stack more pieces of bag plastic on top of the base until it's three layers deep. Put a second piece of baking parchment on top of this pile to protect your iron from the hot plastic. Beginning at one end, iron from the center outward. Press firmly but keep the iron moving. The plastic will shrink as it laminates. Iron just long enough for the plastic to begin to fuse—about 30 to 60 seconds—then slide your parchment along the material to fuse the layers in the next section. Let the material cool. Piece together another layer on top of these three layers to make a total of four layers. Iron to fuse the material as before. Now flip the whole thing over and repeat, ironing the other side of the material. Check the fabric to ensure that it's fully laminated. If it isn't, repeat the ironing.

5 Place pieces of beige plastic shopping bags over the white laminated plastic. The beige plastic should overlap itself randomly in places to create an organic, natural-looking material.

6 Iron and fuse as before. Don't worry if the beige plastic skips a spot, folds, or creases on itself—all of this will add character to your finished piece. Add more scraps as desired for visual interest. Don't forget to hold your "fabric" up to the light to see how it will look when illuminated from behind.

7 Using a straightedge and a craft knife, trim your laminated plastic fabric into a long rectangle measuring about 9 x 30 inches (22.9 x 76.2 cm).

8 Fold down top and bottom "hems" measuring about $1/2$ inch (1.3 cm) along the long edges of the laminated piece. Then iron the fabric using parchment paper to fuse the hem.

9 Roll up the towel and cover it with parchment to create an ironing surface. Bring the ends of your laminated rectangle together, overlapping them by $1/2$ inch (1.3 cm) or so to make a seam, then iron as usual to fuse.

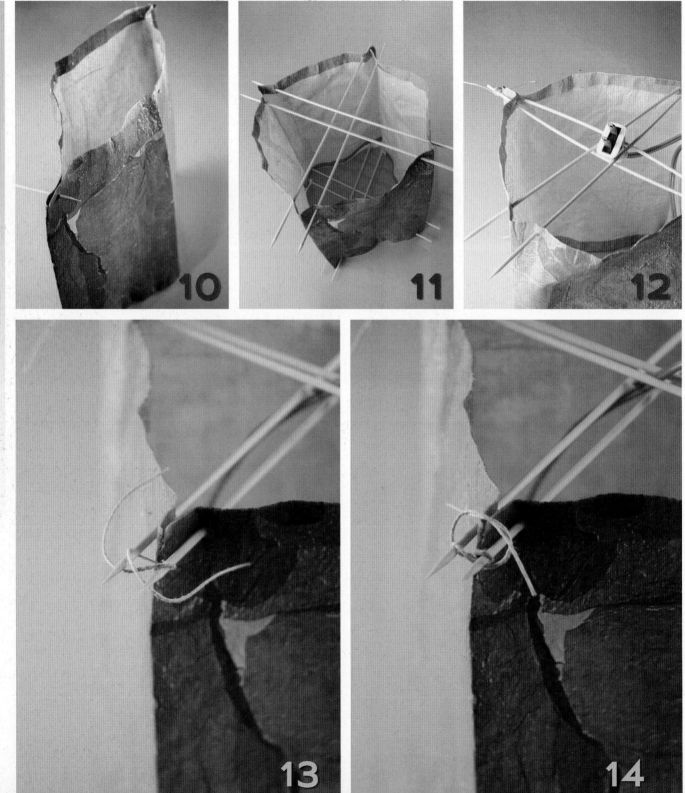

make it (cont.)

10 Fold the lampshade in half and crease it. Using the sharp end of a bamboo skewer, poke a hole through the top hem of the shade about $3/4$ inch (1.9 cm) in from the fold. Repeat this step with the bottom hem and on the opposite end of the shade. Then fold the shade in half along the opposite axis and make holes in the four corners as before.

11 You should now have a square lampshade with two holes in each of the four corners on the top and bottom of the shade. Thread eight bamboo skewers through these corner holes on the diagonal as shown.

12 Feed the lamp socket plug and cord up through the center of the skewer grid as shown.

13 & 14 At each corner, squeeze the bamboo skewers together, folding the corner crease outward. This will force the lampshade into a crisp, rectangular shape. Cut a 6- to 12-inch (15.2 to 30.5 cm) piece of twine and tie it as shown. You can also use thin brass or copper wire to bring the skewer ends together. If desired, cut off the sharp skewer points. Adjust the lampshade as necessary so that it hangs straight and square.

Get Inspired! This is just one of the thousands of things that you can make using fabric created from laminated plastic bags. The material can be thin and flexible or thick and seemingly indestructible, depending on how many layers you laminate together. The color and graphic collage possibilities are endless! What a great way to take noxious litter out of the waste stream and put it to work being stylish and smart. Think day-timer covers, aprons, backpacks, laptop sleeves, baby bibs...

Don't miss the reworked plastic lunch sacks starting on page 60

Totally portable, energy-efficient, and completely charming, these pots of light can transform a mantel, table, or buffet without the worry of fire or the messy wax meltdown of candles. Just pop an LED puck light into a bowl or vase and pile on the glass droplets to make a shimmering, sparkling pool of light that turns on and off with a touch.

POTS *of* LIGHT

MATERIALS

bowls

LED puck lights

glass gems

TOOLS

ADVANTAGE
energy
efficiency

material GREEN TECH

time
1 hour
or less

skill set: *sourcing materials*

BRILLIANT Here's a smart and simple way to put super-efficient LED lights to work in your home. LED lights use just a tiny drop of energy to produce extremely bright, focused light. That intense beam works great for headlights and flashlights but is hardly the stuff of stylish ambience. A jumble of glass beads piled high tames the harsh light and gives it a shimmering, watery glow. Scatter them around on side tables or up steps for your next party. Try clustering them in the center of your table for a magical glow that creates a big buzz while using just a little energy.

BOWLS Just about any bowl, vase, or dish will work for these little pot lights. Make sure your LED puck fits comfortably in the bottom of the bowl with plenty of room left over for the pile of glass drops. Wood bowls add a nice earthy touch to the lights. Antique silver plate adds a glow of its own.

LIGHTS These tiny wireless LED puck lights measure just a few inches across and are available from many manufacturers. They often come in packages of three or more. They use just a watt or two of energy and last tens of thousands of hours. Just push the front of the light on and off.

GLASS GEMS Also known as glass drops, half-marbles, or pebbles, these beads are often used to fill the bottoms of vases or fishbowls and are available at craft, hardware, and decor stores. They come in a rainbow of colors and textures, although dark, rich colors absorb a lot of light. Tumbled or beach glass also works beautifully.

make it

Gather together glass beads and small bowls.

1 Tuck the light in the bottom of the bowl.

2 Pile on the glass beads.

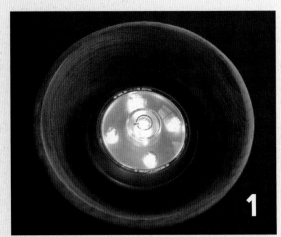

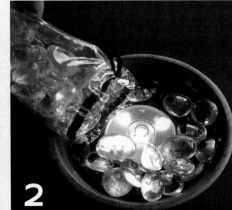

LED lights are super-efficient, using $1/3$ to $1/30$th of the energy used by incandescent and fluorescent bulbs. They have an exceedingly long life of more than 60,000 hours.

CELEBRATE

Timely, lovely, & useful...

Celebrate the beauty and natural

rhythms of every season.

The little red birdhouse was made from a length of old deck railing. The gray house uses a length of barn siding. Look for sound wood that doesn't contain many cracks. If possible, use wood that has paint or stain on just one side—like siding—so that the interior of the house will be untreated.

FOR THE BIRDS

BUILD IT AND THEY WILL COME   What's more exciting than the magical appearance of a nesting pair to set up housekeeping in a new birdhouse? It's especially satisfying to help establish a population of beneficial birds, like swallows, who will return the good deed by helping to keep your yard mosquito-free. These simple birdhouses—made from recycled wood, a few nails, and old license plates—require no special carpentry skills and can be made in less than two hours.

METHOD	material	WOOD	time
salvage			>**3**
skill set:	*simple carpentry*		hours

MATERIALS

salvaged wood board,*
1 x 6 x 36 inches (1.9 x 14 x 91.4 cm)
or
1 x 8 x 36 inches (1.9 x 18.4 x 91.4 cm)

old license plate

galvanized nails

galvanized screws

* Test to be sure old paint is lead free with an inexpensive kit from a home improvement store.

TOOLS

hand or power saw

compass

jigsaw

hole cutter

drill

hammer

pliers

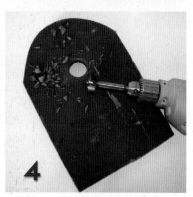

make it

1 Cut two pieces of board, each about 10 x 6 inches (25.4 x 15.2 cm). These will be the front and back of the birdhouse. Then cut three pieces of board, each about 4 x 6 inches (10.1 x 15.2 cm) for the two sides and the bottom.

2 Before you cut the arc that will be the roofline in the front and back, you need to determine how high the sides will be. Measure the long side of one of the side pieces, adding the thickness of the bottom board. Mark this distance up from the bottom on each edge of the front piece. Then use a compass to draw an arch that curves between these two marks. Repeat on the back piece.

3 For the curved roof, cut the curve on the front and back of the house with a jigsaw. For a peaked roof, use a hand saw to make the angled cuts of the roofline.

4 Use a hole cutter in the appropriate size (see examples at right) to drill the entry hole in the center of the front board.

5 You can use screws or nails to attach the pieces. With old wood, it's important to pre-drill the holes, as the wood is more prone to cracks. Start by attaching the bottom to the two sides as shown.

6 Attach the top and back to the U-shaped sides and bottom. Be sure to use galvanized nails or screws with large heads instead of finish nails. I used two on each side and two at the bottom.

7 For the curved roof, gently bend the license plate into an arc, then attach it with a nail or screw (pre-drilled again) at the top of the curve of the house. Add two more nails at intervals down the sloping sides and along the front and back edges for a total of 10 nails. For the peaked roof, bend the license plate over the edge of a table to make a crisp peak. To finish the roof, crimp the edges of the license plate to make a jaunty edge. If needed, drill small holes in the bottom and the sides of the birdhouse for drainage and ventilation.

You can add a decorative piece of wood for a perch if you like, though some experts think that a perch can invite predators.

There's a lot of conflicting advice about the specific attributes of a birdhouse needed to attract specific species. But experts do agree that birds will often surprise you by taking up residence in a house built to the specifications of an entirely different species.

Hole diameter is one of the main features that makes a birdhouse right for one species and not so ideal for another. Check the website of the U.S. Fish and Wildlife Service Office of Migratory Bird Management. It has tips on how to attract specific bird species and where to place birdhouses.

* hole diameters

SWALLOWS (Violet-Green and Tree)	$1^1/_2$ inches (3.8 cm) in diameter
BLUEBIRDS (Eastern, Western, and Mountain)	$1^1/_2$ inches (3.8 cm) in diameter
FLYCATCHERS	$1^1/_2$ to $1^3/_4$ inches (3.8 to 4.4 cm) in diameter
NUTHATCHES	$1^1/_4$ to $1^3/_8$ inches (3.2 to 3.5 cm) in diameter
CHICKADEES	$1^1/_8$ inches (2.9 cm) in diameter

No monoculture here—each of these balls should contain seeds from a variety of plant species native to your area to start an instant, thriving ecosystem. Try to include at least one nitrogen-fixing plant (like soybeans, clover, or alfalfa) in the mix. The seed balls contain everything a seed needs for germination except water, which the spring rain, morning dew, or melting snow should supply.

SEED BALLS

METHOD	material		time
reclaim	EARTH		**1** hour or less

BIOSPHERE Seed balls are tidy packages composed of seeds mixed with dense, fertile compost with a protective jacket of mineral-rich clay. They were pioneered as a way to reclaim waste ground, vacant lots, and fallow, unforgiving soil. These balls are tiny ecosystems contained within well-engineered little delivery systems. The clay keeps the seeds from being blown away, eaten by a bird, or dried out in the sun. Once spring rains melt the clay, the seeds germinate in their own tiny patch of compost. The balls can be sown directly on top of unworked soil—no complex preparation or planting is required.

seeds

compost

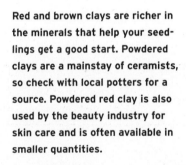

clay

water

MATERIALS

seeds for flowers, herbs,
grasses, or ground cover

good quality compost

powdered clay

water

TOOLS

container for mixing

newspaper

Red and brown clays are richer in the minerals that help your seedlings get a good start. Powdered clays are a mainstay of ceramists, so check with local potters for a source. Powdered red clay is also used by the beauty industry for skin care and is often available in smaller quantities.

make it

Combine two parts mixed seeds with three parts compost in a container. Stir in five parts powdered red or brown clay. Moisten with water and mix with your hands until pliable.

Now you're ready to roll. Pinch off a penny-sized hunk of the clay mixture and roll it between the palms of your hands until it forms into a tight ball. The sphere should be about $3/4$ inches (1.9 cm) in diameter. Set the balls on a newspaper and allow them to dry for 24 to 48 hours, then store in a cool, dry place until ready to sow.

Lay out seed balls in late winter or early spring at a density of about 10 or more per square yard (.83 square meter.) They will germinate when the time is right.

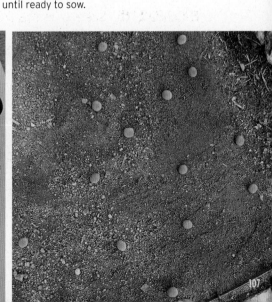

MUSIC BOXES

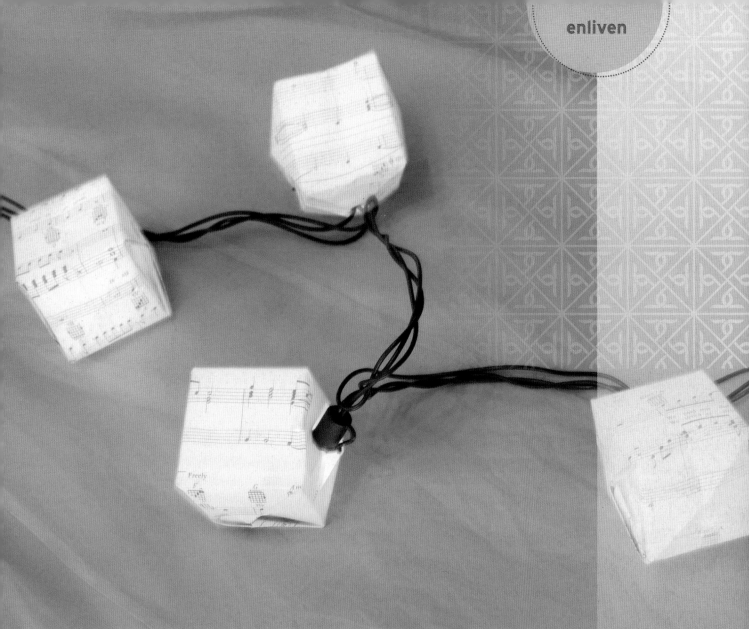

DO YOURSELF A LITTLE FAVOR Add a festive touch to your next celebration with these origami boxes made from recycled paper. Stuffed with sweet treats, they're perfect little party favors. They can also be strung onto a strand of super-efficient LED lights to make lyrical lanterns perfect for hanging or using as your table's centerpiece. These boxes are made with recycled sheet music to add a celebratory tone, but pages from a discarded book would be just as lovely.

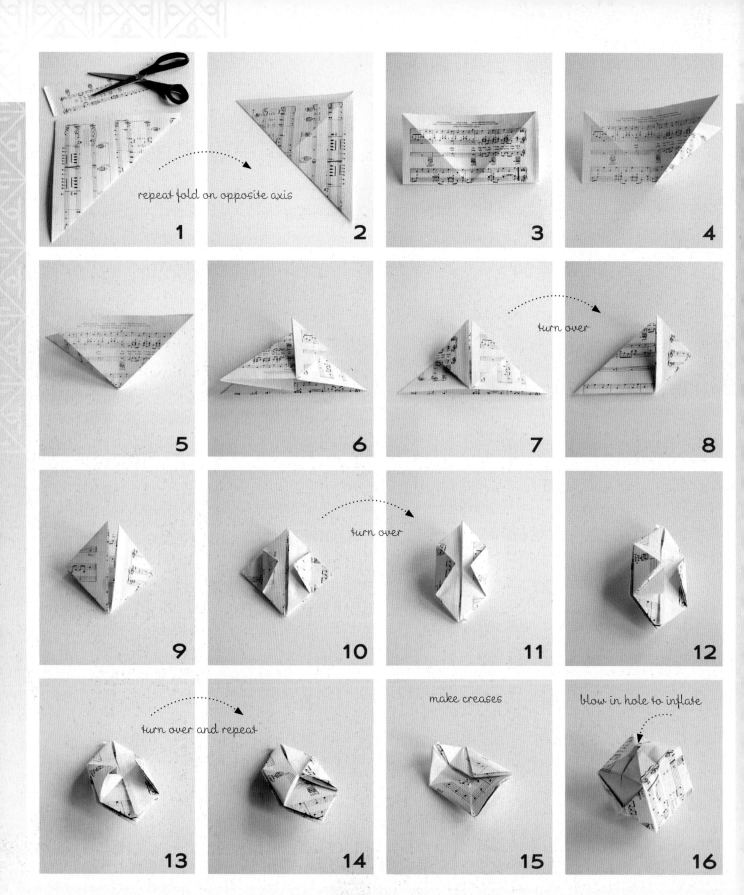

repeat fold on opposite axis

1

2

3

4

5

6

7

turn over

8

9

turn over

10

11

12

turn over and repeat

13

14

make creases

15

blow in hole to inflate

16

METHOD
recycle

material BOOKS·

time
1 hour
or less

skill set: *folding*

MATERIALS

sheet music

LED string lights* or treats for filling

make it

A PICTURE IS WORTH 1000 WORDS
Sixteen pictures may be just enough
to teach you how to make this origami
box. It's easy once you get started.
And the final step, when you inflate
the box as though blowing up a bal-
loon, is absolute magic. Give it a try.

To string the boxes onto LED lights,
simply ease the bulb into the box
through the hole you used for inflat-
ing. Work slowly, and the bulb should
slide in with no tearing. To fill your box
with treats as party favors, use the
same technique. Depending on the
sizes of the treats, they should come
out easily without opening the box.
The box can also be torn open like a
miniature present.

 * IMPORTANT! Do not use regular
 strings of incandescent lights for this
 project. They are much less energy-
 efficient than LED lights, generating
 enough heat to become a fire hazard.

A lovely, graceful centerpiece that won't hide one dinner guest from another, this trough-style vase can hold endless combinations of dried flora. Autumn leaves make an intriguing arrangement, as does a forest of twigs or grasses.

FALL LINE-UP

CUT AND DRIED As green foliage turns to brown and seeds take flight, autumnal plants are at their most sculptural. This linear vase relies on two dimensions to highlight the intriguing shapes of seedpods and the armature of vegetation. Simply constructed from a 1 x 4 piece of beetle-kill pine and held together with bolts and wing nuts, the narrow trough can be filled with florist's foam to hold the dry plants. Or better yet, line up polystyrene foam peanuts that can be replaced with the next arrangement. Use your imagination and an obliging meadow or garden for plant material. Experiment! The combinations and permutations are endless. If the aesthetic of the foam peanuts offends, cover them with a layer of sand or grass seed.

METHOD: reconsider | material: **WEEDS** | time: **>3** hours
skill set: *carpentry*

MATERIALS

1 x 4 (1.9 x 8.9 cm) board
about 72 inches (182.9 cm) long

paint

cabinetmaker's wax

four wood bolts, each 3 inches (7.6 cm),
with wing nuts to match

polystyrene foam peanuts

small sheet of cork, $^1/_4$ inch (0.6 cm) thick

small nails or brads

TOOLS

hand or power saw

rag for rubbing on paint and wax

clamp

drill

craft knife to cut cork

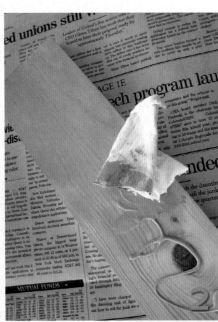

make it

1 The vase can be made whatever length fits your display area or table. This version uses two 1 x 4 x 28-inch (1.9 x 8.9 x 71.1 cm) boards and two 1 x 4 x 3-inch (1.9 x 8.9 x 7.6 cm) end spacers.

2 You can leave the wood raw or finish it with a non-toxic sealer. I rubbed on a thin coat of sea-green latex paint, then let it dry before buffing the vase with cabinetmaker's wax.

3 Sandwich the spacers between the two long boards and clamp. Drill a hole through all three layers at the top and bottom of each end for the 3-inch (7.6 cm) bolts. Thread the bolts through the holes and attach the wing nuts.

4 Cut a strip of cork to cover the bottom of your vase. Attach the strip to the bottom of the box with tiny brads. This holds the foam and plant material in place and protects your tabletop from scratches. Be sure to sink the nail heads slightly into the cork.

5 A variety of materials can be used to fill the channel and make it easy to poke in plant stems. You can cut a piece of florist's foam to size, or—if you are feeling extremely green—recycle some foam peanuts to do the job (as shown here).

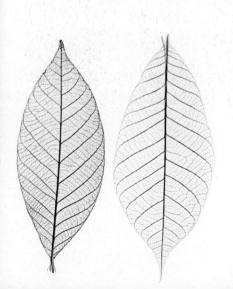

ORNAMENTAL METAL

MATERIALS

aluminum soda-pop cans

copper or brass wire

miscellaneous
large-holed
beads

TOOLS

craft scissors

gloves

cellophane tape

hammer

cardboard

pushpin or small nail

needle-nose pliers

CAN CAN Who says holiday ornaments have to be made from precious materials? Maybe the most beautiful thing is the transformation of something humble into something grand. These sweet, clever ornaments started their lives as soda-pop cans, but after a few snips with scissors, whacks with a hammer, and a thoroughly prickly exchange with a thumbtack, they're the perfect silvery specimens for the tree or anything else that needs a little extra sparkle this season.

METHOD: recycle | material: ALUMINUM | time: 1 hour or less

skill set: cutting and piercing

make it

1 Using ordinary craft scissors, cut the bottom and top off a soda can to render a flat sheet of aluminum. Be sure to wear gloves while cutting the aluminum, as the edges can be sharp. Roll the sheet back on itself if you need to so that the aluminum will lay flat.

2 Create a square or diamond-shaped template out of paper, then tape it to your sheet of aluminum and cut out two pieces.

3 Cut about $3/16$ inch (0.5 cm) off all the edges of one of the cut pieces. Put the two pieces together with the printed sides to the inside. Notch the edges of the larger as shown in the picture. This will make a neat, flat corner for your finished ornament.

4 Fold the edge of the bigger piece over that of the smaller. Tap along the edge with a small hammer to create a crisp fold.

5 Place a piece of cardboard under your ornament and pierce the metal with a sturdy pushpin to create the punched pattern. You can freehand the design or draw it on in advance with a soft pencil. Try to pierce all the way around the border of your piece first, as this will "sew" the two pieces of metal together.

6 & 7 Cut a 4-inch (10.1 cm) piece of thin wire and thread it through the hole at the top of the ornament. Twist to secure. Then string a few pretty beads on the wire for color and make a curlicue at the top. The curlicue will hold everything in place and create an easy way for you to hang your new ornament on the tree.

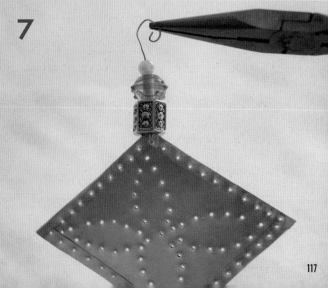

MAGAZINE SHAPES

Look for brightly colored, glossy pages—the best kind are pages that have lots of color on both sides.

JUMP OFF THE PAGE Recycle some of the old magazines and catalogs that clutter your shelves into a one-of-a-kind, out-of-the-ordinary holiday ornament. Simply cut circles and squares from discarded publications, stack and staple them, then unfold them into jewel-bright spheres and diamonds.

The diamonds are made just like the spheres, but you start with 2- to 3-inch (5 to 7 cm) squares in order to make them. Both the fold and the staple are done on the diagonal.

1

2

3

make it

1 Cut 3-inch (7.6 cm) circles out of pages using a circle cutter. You can also use a glass or lid as a template and draw a line for cutting along with scissors.

2 Stack 20 to 30 circles together. Fold the top one in half, then unfold. That fold line will tell you where to position your staple. One staple in the middle should pin all the circles together.

3 Unfold the stapled stack, fanning each sheaf of paper as you go until you have a symmetrical sphere. Poke a hole with a needle through all the layers at the top of the stack and hang with a thread or wire.

METHOD	material	time
recycle	MAGAZINES	**1** hour or less
skill set: *cutting and folding*		

MATERIALS

old magazines, catalogs, brochures or calendars

thread or wire for hanging

TOOLS

circle cutter or scissors

stapler

needle or hole punch

BY THE BOOK

LITERARY FIGURES Here's a supremely simple and fun

way to recycle a hardcover book into an

erudite holiday decoration.

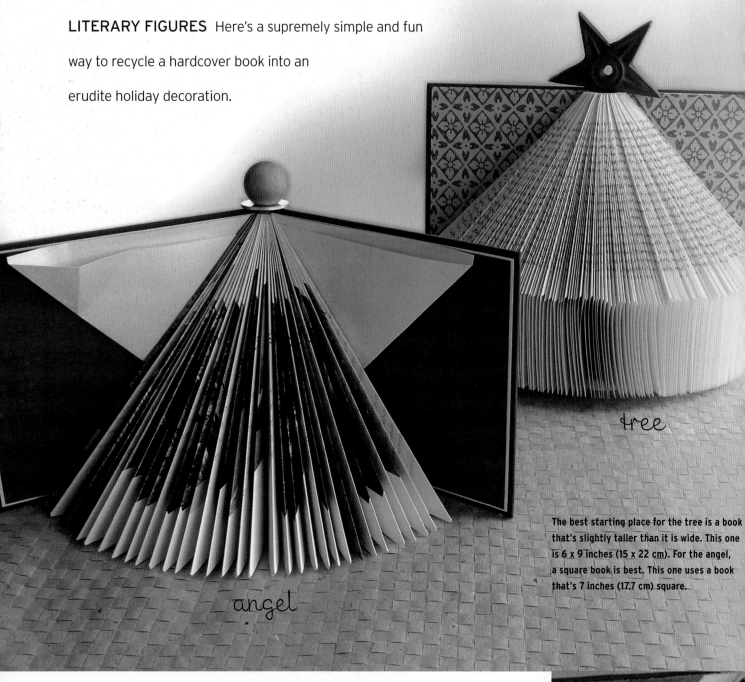

tree

angel

The best starting place for the tree is a book
that's slightly taller than it is wide. This one
is 6 x 9 inches (15 x 22 cm). For the angel,
a square book is best. This one uses a book
that's 7 inches (17.7 cm) square.

METHOD	material	BOOKS	time
recycle			**1** hour or less
skill set: *folding*			

MATERIALS

hardcover books

decorative paper
for end sheets

glue stick

small eyehook

metal washer

wooden knob

metal star

beeswax

TOOLS

ruler

scissors

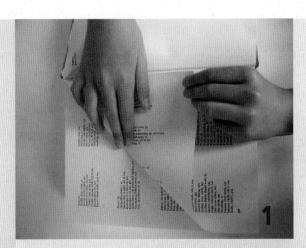

make it

1 Fold the pages from the top outside corner down until the top edge of the page is tangent to the spine of the book. Crease with your finger.

2 If your book isn't blessed with beautiful end papers (the paper on the inside front and back covers), add something special of your own. Measure and cut the paper, then adhere it with a glue stick.

3 In the photo opposite, the angel's wings are creamy white against the olive green inside cover of the book. To make the wings, fold the book's first and last pages in the opposite direction as the rest of the book.

4 To make the angel's stylized head, insert a small eyehook into the pocket where the book spine meets the hard cover. Add a brass washer, then a simple wooden knob. A spot of beeswax or clay will hold the knob in place on top of the washer.

If you'd like to make the Christmas tree, the natural pocket formed at the top of a book's spine makes a perfect holder for a vintage iron star. Stars like this one were used extensively in brick and mortar construction in centuries past and can be found at antique and junk stores.

WRAPPED UP

An old paper shopping bag gets spruced up with simple prints made from a metal washer you can buy at the hardware store. The purple dot is made with a pencil eraser dipped in paint. The bow is simply three loops of heavyweight paper stapled in the middle and decorated with a bottle cap.

METHOD	material	time
reconfigure	PAPER	1 hour or less
skill set:	printing, cutting, etc	

IT'S A WRAP We're making a list, checking it twice . . . then we're staying up past midnight begrudgingly wrapping gifts in sheets of overpriced flocked finery that we top with bows made in a sweatshop in China and tags that are as personal as an appointment reminder from the dentist. But all that's about to change. Check out the works of art that you can whip up with just a few humble materials and simple craft techniques, like the following: recycled newsprint, paper bags, manila envelopes that are crumpled so they resemble Florentine fabric, easy-to-do block printing, beautiful, colorful, eclectic wallpapers cut from discarded sample books, raffia, hemp, and jute string, an intriguing pastiche of baubles and beads, and old soda-pop caps.

MATERIALS

large sheets of paper to recycle:
newspaper, paper bags, tissue paper

craft paints in various colors,
including metallics

cover-weight paper for tags and bows

raffia, jute, or hemp string

bottle caps

TOOLS

scissors

pinking shears

stapler

hole punch

paper plate for paint

drill to make holes in bottle caps

You can use all kinds of things to make a print: a potato or apple can be cut into a simple shape to make a printing block. Even a rolled scroll of paper makes a print when the edge is dipped in paint (see above right).

CRUSHED PAPER

Transform paper that looks unfashionably utilitarian into something that has a handmade texture resembling crushed silk. Paper that would otherwise be too stiff to use as wrapping can be crumpled and crushed to make a soft paper that wraps beautifully and defies its roots. The secret is to ball up the paper first, then unroll it, then crumple it repeatedly until it crushes easily into a small ball. Unroll it, smooth it out, and it's ready to wrap.

What to recycle

newspaper or newsprint	plain white bond paper
brown paper bags	old sheet music
craft paper	maps
manila envelopes	last year's wrapping paper
wallpaper scraps	old books

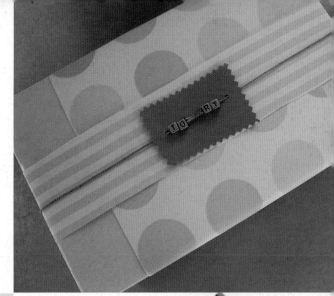

RECYCLED WALLPAPER SCRAPS

Wallpaper comes in a dizzying array of colors, patterns, and materials. Many papers are designed to look beautiful together—they share the same palette and are made for mixing and matching. This makes them ideal for decorating packages. You can use a wide swath of floral paper to wrap the package, then cut a thin band of striped paper to make a color-coordinated ribbon. Then cut out a paisley or a medallion to decorate the tag. Because wallpaper patterns change with each new season, wallpaper sample books are frequently tossed in the dumpster, so they're free for the taking. Look for books full of more "papery" wallpaper, rather than the kind that's vinyl-coated and too thick or stiff to use for wrapping presents.

Where to find wallpaper samples

wallpaper and paint stores
interior decorators
some fabric shops

BAUBLES, BEADS, AND TAGS

Use your imagination to top off a package: You can raid the junk drawer, the hardware aisle, the bead and button jar, and the recycling bin to find lots of beautiful baubles to decorate your gifts. For personalizing packages, keep a rubber stamp alphabet or letter stickers on hand. A fun trick: Recycle the postmarked stamp from mailed envelopes to make tags (see photo at center right).

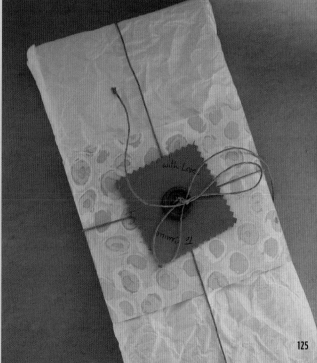

What to try

old game pieces	brass washers
antique keys	fancy brads
seashells	tags and stickers from the office supply store
large metal and glass beads	
alphabet beads	string
pop bottle tops	raffia

THANKS

MY LONG LIST OF ACKNOWLEDGMENTS

must begin with LINDA LIGON. As publisher and founder of *Natural Home* magazine, she launched me into all this eco-crafting stuff almost 10 years ago. She is the reason this book is in your hands right now. Linda will blush and scoff at that idea, but I can hardly think of a single event in my career as a writer and designer in which she didn't play a role—either as mentor, cheerleader, client, confidante, or fairy godmother.

Thanks to my dad, RON HARRIS, a truly inspired engineer and master tinkerer who is blessed with an unerring grasp of spatial relationships and an unnervingly vast knowledge of artisan tools and craftsman techniques. Even more important, his keen sense of the absurd and his impish delight in Rube Goldberg-ing make him my most indispensable co-conspirator.

A huge heartfelt thanks to my husband, TOM WASINGER, who was willing to be my sawyer, hauler, and gofer even while scratching his head over my latest crazy scheme. And to my eco-savvy children, CAMILLE and RAINER, who put up with sawdust, duct tape scraps, and heaps of milk jugs and baby food jars constantly piled up in the sink, who acted as muses and models for me at all hours of the day and night, and were always lavish with their ideas and encouragement.

Thanks also to Marlies Harris, Eliza Kuelthau, Craig Hansen, Rolland Fischer, DeAnn and Bill Snyder, Frank Riegel, Willy Sutton, Michael Signorella, Robyn Lawrence, Bryan Welch, Rebecca DiDomenico, Deborah K. Jones, Scott and Joellen Raderstorf, Nini Coleman, Mickey Houlihan, Isabelle Tierney, Pardis Amirshahi, Ed Pierson, and Bridget Johnson (The Green Girl), all of whom have inspired and cajoled, brainstormed and schemed, lent ears and hands all at the right time and in the right measure.

Thanks to the crew at Lark Books—Paige Gilchrist, Kathy Sheldon, Julie Hale, Chris Bryant, Nicole McConville, and countless others—who were all patience, encouragement, wisdom, and competence throughout the long, complicated process of making a book (and they are really fun to work with, too!).

INDEX